T0182562

SALINGER'S SOUL

His Personal & Religious Odyssey

SALINGER'S SOUL

Stephen B. Shepard

A POST HILL PRESS BOOK
ISBN: 979-8-88845-472-5
ISBN (eBook): 979-8-88845-473-2

Salinger's Soul:
His Personal & Religious Odyssey
© 2024 by Stephen B. Shepard
All Rights Reserved

Cover design by Cody Corcoran
Cover photo by Lotte Jacobi, 1950

Post Hill Press
New York • Nashville
posthillpress.com

Published in the United States of America
1 2 3 4 5 6 7 8 9 10

For my family, as always:

Lynn, Sarah and Matt, Ned and Libeth, Jake and Charlie.

TABLE OF CONTENTS

Introduction 9

Chapter 1: "All That David Copperfield Kind
          of Crap" 13

Chapter 2: The Mentor on Morningside Heights..... 22

Chapter 3: Salinger at War 31

Chapter 4: The German Connection......................... 47

Chapter 5: Jerry and His War Bride......................... 51

Chapter 6: "Tall, Dark, and Handsome" 56

Chapter 7: Here at *The New Yorker*....................... 63

Chapter 8: Holden in the Rye.................................. 83

Chapter 9: From Seymour to Teddy 96

Chapter 10: Retreat to Cornish 103

Chapter 11: Religious Zeal.................................... 117

Chapter 12: "To See God"................................... 132

Chapter 13: "The Last Minutes of Her Girlhood" ... 139

Chapter 14: Sightings and Skirmishes.................... 155

Chapter 15: Father Figure 172

Chapter 16: Salinger's Legacy............................... 184

Appendix 192
Selected Bibliography (in chronological order) 200
Endnotes... 202
Index 221
Acknowledgments.. 231
About the Author.. 234

INTRODUCTION

Jerome David Salinger remains one of our best-known but least-understood writers.

Called Sonny by his parents, Jerry by his friends, and J. D. Salinger by the rest of the world, he wrote *The Catcher in the Rye* in 1951, one of the most iconic American novels of the twentieth century. Some two hundred thousand copies are still sold every year, bringing the worldwide total to more than sixty-five million—one of the best-selling books of all time.[1] He was thirty-two when the book was published.

Salinger dropped out of public view two years later. He retreated to Cornish, New Hampshire, a rural hamlet some 250 miles from New York City. He continued writing nearly every day, but never published anything after 1965. He lived mostly in seclusion for the rest of his life, becoming famous for not wanting to be famous.

His story, however, is not over. His son, Matt, has been sorting through the unpublished writing Salinger left behind after his death in 2010. "My father was writing for nearly 50 years without publishing," Matt told *The Guardian* in 2019, on the centenary of Salinger's birth. "That's a lot of material." Much of it is rumored to be short stories and perhaps another novel or two. At least some of it will likely be released within the next couple of years.[2]

Just imagine: The chance to read the stories Salinger had written in his years of retreat, then locked away in a vault somewhere—the very expression of his self-exile.

It will be a literary event of enormous magnitude.

Salinger's newly released fiction will have special resonance for me. In 2018, I wrote a book called *A Literary Journey to Jewish Identity: Re-Reading Bellow, Roth, Malamud, Ozick, and Other Great Jewish Writers*. At first, I thought of including Salinger, but I quickly realized his Jewishness was a complicated saga, the transition of a bar mitzvah boy in New York to a practitioner of Eastern religions who shed all traces of the Judaism of his youth.

There is nothing the least bit Jewish about Holden Caulfield, his most famous fictional character, in the book that thrust fame on the reluctant Salinger. Nor is there anything much Jewish in the later Glass stories, even though Seymour, Franny, Zooey, and the other Glass siblings had a Jewish father, like Salinger himself.

Yet Salinger continued to fascinate me. As the COVID pandemic sidelined all of us, I began reading much of what was written about Salinger over the years: the biographies, the scholarly papers, the magazine profiles, the memoirs of those who knew him. There was plenty there, and I learned an enormous amount about his literary work and something of his reclusive life.

But I sensed something missing: a deeper understanding of the man and his personal journey. I realized, for instance, how little I knew about the trauma Salinger experienced during World War II, from landing at Normandy on D-Day to helping liberate a Nazi concentration camp ten months later. Or that he suffered a nervous breakdown soon after the war ended and was hospitalized in Germany. Or that he married a German woman and tried to pass her off as French when he brought her home to his parents' apartment on Park Avenue. Or that he harbored a lifelong obsession with young women, including affairs with women twenty, thirty, or even forty years younger.

How did it all add up? How did it influence his life and work?

By many accounts, Salinger remained depressed, on and off, for much of his life. He sought solace in various Eastern religions—from Zen Buddhism to mystical Hinduism—that he practiced in his daily life and showcased in his later fiction, especially in the Glass stories. Though Salinger was never labeled a "Jewish writer," as were such contemporaries as Saul Bellow, Bernard Malamud, and Philip Roth, he certainly became a religious writer.

Eventually, Salinger's religious focus turned to Vedanta, a mystical form of Hinduism. He embraced it with the passion of a true believer, meditating daily and studying the sacred texts of the religion. It was Vedanta, preaching against acts of personal ego, that influenced his decision to stop publishing anything after 1965. For Salinger, writing was necessary, but he came to believe that putting his name on a story or book and offering it for sale to all comers was an intolerable bid for publicity, surely an act of ego.

Yet Salinger broke with Vedantic practice in one crucial respect. He didn't heed its dictum to lead a life of celibacy.[3] Instead, Salinger was obsessed by post-adolescent women: those, as one of his fictional characters put it, "in the last minute of her girlhood."[4]

When Salinger's decades of unpublished writing finally come to light in the next couple of years, his fiction will merit review in the context of his personal experiences at the time. Building on what has been written earlier by scholars and biographers, I've synthesized and reinterpreted Salinger's life and how it affected his literature. I hope I've provided a revealing look at his personal and religious odyssey: the background for the new stories that lie just ahead.

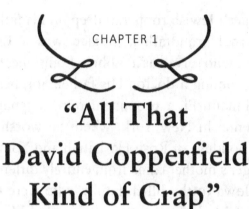

CHAPTER 1

"All That David Copperfield Kind of Crap"

*If you really want to hear about it, the first
thing you'll probably want to know is where
I was born and what my lousy childhood was
like, and how my parents were occupied and
all before they had me, and all that David
Copperfield kind of crap, but I don't feel like
going into it, if you want to know the truth.*

—HOLDEN CAULFIELD, *The Catcher in the Rye*

J. D. Salinger said and wrote little of his own background, but we do know many basic facts about his early life. He was born in New York on January 1, 1919, the second of two children. His sister, Doris, who became a buyer in the dress department at Bloomingdale's, was six years older. "In a Jewish family a boy is special," she recalled years later. "Mother doted on him. He could do no wrong."[5]

Salinger's Jewish roots ran deep on his father's side. His paternal grandfather, in fact, was a Lithuanian immigrant who served as a rabbi in Louisville, Kentucky, before becoming a doctor. His father, Sol, belonged to Temple Emanu-El, a prominent reform synagogue on Fifth Avenue in New York, where he worshipped on the high holidays of Rosh Hashanah and Yom Kippur.[6]

Salinger's mother came from entirely different stock. Born in Iowa to the Jillich family, who were Catholics of Scotch/Irish descent, she was christened Marie. When she married Sol, she changed her name to the more Jewish-sounding Miriam (Moses's sister). As Miriam Salinger, she "passed" as Jewish—no small irony in pre-war America. Sonny didn't find out his mother wasn't Jewish until well past his thirteenth birthday—after his bar mitzvah.[7]

Once he learned his mother wasn't the Jew she pretended to be, Salinger was quick to abandon his own Jewishness. In so doing, he simultaneously curbed his identification with his hard-to-please Jewish father and embraced the identity of his much-adored Gentile mother. He had won his Oedipal battle.

The Salinger family lived in the Jewish section of upper Harlem when Sonny was born, then moved to 113th Street and Broadway, near Columbia University, then to West 82nd Street, not far from the American Museum of Natural History. He attended a local public school, P.S. 166, where his IQ was recorded as 104, barely above average.[8]

His father worked for J. S. Hoffman & Company, known as Hofco, an importer of cheeses and pork products, becoming general manager of Hofco's New York office. As Sol's business prospered, the family moved again, just after Jerry's bar mitzvah, this time to a tonier apartment building, 1133 Park Avenue at 91st Street. It was a comfortable life, even during the Depression, and the family often had a live-in maid. Every summer, Jerry went to Camp Wigwam in Maine, where he, an aspiring thespian, was voted "most popular actor." Jerry remained close to Miriam all his life and dedicated *The Catcher in the Rye* "To My Mother." But he often clashed with his father, who wanted him to join the family business and later disdained Jerry's goal of becoming a writer.[9]

Sol, more a social climber than an observant Jew, became eager to assimilate into mainstream America, meaning WASP America. He transferred Jerry out of P.S. 166, where most of the students were Jewish, enrolling him at the McBurney School, a fashionable private school in New York, which was affiliated with the YMCA, the *C* very much part of the attraction.

As Mark Twain once said of himself, Salinger never let his schooling interfere with his education. Eager to engage in extracurricular activities at McBurney, Jerry managed the fencing team, wrote for the school newspaper, and acted in school plays. But his grades were so poor that he was expelled from McBurney within two years. According to school records, Jerry's grades in his second year at McBurney were 72 in English, 70 in German, 68 in geometry, and F in Latin.[10]

The McBurney School made a brief appearance in *The Catcher in the Rye*. It was the school that was scheduled to have a fencing match with Pencey Prep, Holden Caulfield's boarding school. The match was cancelled because Holden left the foils on a New York subway train, a fictional replay of what had happened to Jerry at McBurney.

After Jerry flunked out of McBurney, Sol dispatched him to Valley Forge Military Academy in Pennsylvania, where the students were all boys (a matter of principle) and nearly all Gentiles (a matter of habit). At first, the family had some concern that Jerry would face anti-Semitism at Valley Forge, so much so that he was accompanied for his admissions interview only by his mother because, it was thought, his father looked too Jewish.[11] In fact, Salinger's sister Doris did think "he suffered terribly from anti-Semitism when he went away to military school,"[12] but there is nothing in Salinger's own writing or in any of the writing about him that suggests he faced discrimination at the school.

Salinger attended Valley Forge from 1934 to 1936. Located in Wayne, Pennsylvania, about twenty miles from Philadelphia, it was very much a military academy. The students, known as cadets, wore uniforms and marched in formation, often armed with rifles. The entire campus was fenced, and the gate was patrolled by cadets.

Stripped of some of its militarism, Valley Forge ultimately became the model for Pencey Prep. But unlike Holden, who flunked out of Pencey Prep, Jerry Salinger benefited from the military discipline at Valley Forge, turning into a decent student who made friends and participated in many school activities, from the Glee Club to the Mask and Spur drama society. He became the literary editor at his class yearbook, *Crossed Sabres*, even writing his class anthem, sung at graduation ceremonies for many years thereafter. Here are the last four lines of his farewell ode for the Class of 1936:[13]

> "...*Goodbyes are said, we march ahead,*
> *Success we go to find.*
> *Our forms are gone from Valley Forge:*
> *Our hearts are left behind."*

It was at Valley Forge that Salinger, who harbored ambitions to be a writer, began writing short stories, often working at night with a flashlight under his blanket.[14]

Salinger's time at Valley Forge had another, unexpected, benefit. He befriended a classmate named William Faison, whose sister, Elizabeth Murray, soon became a confidante of Salinger's. It was Murray, in 1938, who told Salinger to read F. Scott Fitzgerald's *The Great Gatsby*. At nineteen, he had never heard of the book or its author.[15] Though Murray was a dozen years older than Salinger, had two children, and lived in Brielle, New Jersey, they corresponded regularly from 1940 to 1963. Salinger, who valued her advice, sometimes sent along portions of his manuscripts. In 1968, Murray sold thirty-eight of Salinger's letters, plus some manuscripts, to the Harry Ransom Center at the University of Texas in Austin, where they are available to scholars. The letters, especially the early ones, "show Salinger maturing into a serious writer," according to the Center's magazine.[16] When Murray died in 1979, Salinger wrote a tender letter to her daughter, Gloria, recalling Murray as an "astonishingly true and vital and rallying and encouraging friend."[17]

Salinger reverted to his bad old ways in college, spending less than a semester at NYU's Washington Square campus in Greenwich Village. He skipped classes, ignored his assignments, and dropped out before he was pushed out.

His father, hoping that he would join the family business, sent him to Europe to work for his partner. Jerry, of course, was not the least bit interested in joining his father's cheese-and-meat emporium. And Sol's business practices in the 1930s were hardly admirable. He was vice president of Hofco when the company was indicted several times in the early 1940s for price fixing and violation of US antitrust laws. Ultimately, Hofco pleaded no contest to some of the charges and paid relatively small fines. It also agreed to stop labeling Swiss cheese in a way that implied the Wisconsin-produced cheese was made in Switzerland.[18]

• • •

Though Jerry Salinger learned little about the cheese business in Europe, he spent nearly a year there starting in April 1937, mostly in Austria amid the gathering clouds of war. It was in Vienna that he became fluent in German, which proved valuable when he served in the army during the war.

Most of his time in Vienna he lived with a family in the Jewish quarter whose daughter became a good friend—and probably a romantic partner. Salinger left Vienna for the US on March 9, 1938, just days before the Nazis annexed Austria. Within a week of his homecoming, the *New York Times* had run two stories describing how the Nazis forced Jews to scrub streets in Vienna to get rid of anti-Nazi slogans left by the previous regime.[19]

Salinger never forgot the girl. In 1945, as the war was ending, he wrote a letter to Ernest Hemingway (whom he had befriended in Paris after the liberation), saying he hoped the army would send him to Vienna where he wanted "to put a pair of ice skates on the feet of a Viennese girl I knew."[20] It was only after the war ended that Salinger did go back to Vienna, only to discover that the entire family had been killed by the Nazis.

What we know about this tragic episode comes largely from a short story Salinger wrote, appropriately called "A Girl I Knew," published in the February 1948 issue of *Good Housekeeping*. It is the only one of Salinger's surviving stories that is based on his time in Vienna, and the only Salinger story that dealt with the Holocaust.

In Salinger's fictionalized account, he is John, a college dropout who falls in love with Leah, who lives in the same Vienna apartment house he did. "She was 16 and beautiful," John says, "...She had immense eyes that always seemed in danger of capsizing in their own innocence...she was probably the first appreciable thing of beauty I had seen that struck me as being wholly legitimate."

After the war, John returns to visit his old pre-war building, now occupied by American military officers. He asks the staff sergeant on duty about Leah, the girl he once knew who was later killed at Buchenwald. The sergeant responds with callous indifference: "Yeah? What was she, a Jew or something?"[21]

Leah thus represents something more than a Holocaust victim. She symbolizes the indifference of the broader population, even an army sergeant, that helped make the Holocaust possible in the first place.

● ● ●

After his stay in Vienna, Salinger again tried college, this time in 1938 at Ursinus College, a small coed school in Pennsylvania founded after the Civil War by the German Reformed Church. Some of his classmates remember him walking around campus in a black chesterfield overcoat with a velvet collar.[22] One classmate, Franny Glassmoyer (the obvious namesake for Franny Glass in Salinger's later fiction) remembers him as "a loner" and "a critic."[23]

Salinger didn't fare any better at Ursinus than he had at NYU. He left Ursinus after just nine weeks. He didn't flunk out. He just walked away without telling anyone.[24] In his brief stay, he did manage to write for the college newspaper, the *Ursinus Weekly*, including a column that explained his reasons for enrolling at Ursinus: "Once there was a young man who...did not want to go to work for his Daddykins—or any other unreasonable man. So the young man went back to college."[25]

He also reviewed plays produced at Ursinus, and he fancied himself a theater critic for *The New Yorker*. Or perhaps making it on Broadway or Hollywood as writer, actor, or producer. But writing fiction prevailed: it was at Ursinus that he declared his goal of becoming a major writer. He even boasted to classmates that he would someday write the Great American Novel.[26]

A dozen years later, *The Catcher in the Rye* was published.

CHAPTER 2

The Mentor on
Morningside Heights

To fulfill his lofty ambitions, Salinger signed up for a couple of night courses in the spring semester of 1939 at Columbia University's School of General Studies, then known as the Extension Division. One course changed his life: a short-story writing class taught by Whit Burnett, a lanky thirty-nine-year-old adjunct professor who was the editor of *Story* magazine, a well-respected quarterly that frequently published short stories by aspiring young writers.[27]

Burnett and his then-wife, Martha Foley, had founded *Story* magazine in 1931, six years after they met at the *San Francisco Journal*, where both were reporters. They were polar opposites—she lively and outgoing, he laconic and introverted—but they fell in love and soon married. Later they traveled and worked in Europe, writing short stories as well as news articles. In Vienna, Foley came up with the idea of starting their own magazine to publish short stories by little-known writers. Burnett was skeptical, but he agreed to sign on. They produced their first issue of *Story* in April 1931, turning out 167 copies on a mimeograph machine at the Foreign Correspondents' Club in Vienna.

In the ensuing years, they discovered Nelson Algren, William Saroyan, John Cheever, and Carson McCullers—a list that would soon expand to include Richard Wright, Joseph Heller, Truman Capote, Tennessee Williams, and Norman Mailer, whose pen name at the time was Norman Kingsley Mailer.

Salinger started out in Burnett's Columbia course as academically listless as he had ever been at NYU or Ursinus College, sitting in the back row of room 505 in what is now called Dodge Hall, staring out the window, as Burnett later recalled. But he re-enrolled in the course for a second semester, and this time something clicked in Salinger. He submitted several stories to Burnett, who was amazed to discover that the indifferent student in the back row was a talented writer.[28]

Burnett became Salinger's mentor. In its spring 1940 edition, *Story* magazine published a Salinger story called "The Young Folks," which takes place at a party of twenty-somethings, a WASPy crowd that downs plenty of Scotch, chain-smokes cigarettes, and talks of years at Princeton. Even in this early story, Salinger's talent was evident, as in his description of the party's hostess:

> "Lucille Henderson sighed as heavily as
> her dress would allow, and then, knit-

ting what there was of her brow, gazed about the room at the noisy young people she had invited to drink up her father's Scotch."[29]

The plot consists largely of a conversation between an unpopular woman, Edna Phillips, and an upper-class guy, William Jameson, Jr., the object of her affection. But he's more interested in a blond woman at the same party and resists Edna's overtures. The story showcases Salinger's emerging gift for telling a story through dialogue, capturing the essence of his characters by what they said. Re-reading it now, I feel as if the story had been written by a playwright:

> Edna: "It isn't that I can't appreciate how a boy feels after he dates you all summer and spends money he hasn't any right to spend on theater tickets and night spots and all. I mean, I can understand. He feels you owe him something. Well, I'm not that way…It's gotta be the real thing with me…I mean love and all."
>
> Jameson: "Yeah. Look, uh. I really oughtta get going. I got this theme for Monday. Hell, I shoulda been home hours ago. So I think I'll go in and get a drink and get goin.'"[30]

Salinger was paid twenty-five dollars for "The Young Folks," his first published story and the only one carrying the byline of Jerome Salinger. He was J. D. Salinger from then on. "I don't know why I write under the initials J. D.," Salinger wrote to Burnett on September 6, 1940. "Jerome was a lousy name. It always sounds so much like Jerome."[31]

After "The Young Folks" appeared, a few literary agents reached out to Salinger, offering their services. He picked the Harold Ober Literary Agency, which just happened to represent F. Scott Fitzgerald, who had become a recent favorite of Salinger's. Ober assigned the rookie writer to a young woman named Dorothy Olding. She remained his agent for the next fifty years.

Burnett published another of Salinger's stories two years later, a dark, rather undistinguished story called "The Long Debut of Lois Taggett," which again focused on upper-class young people, this time with more explicit criticism. Lois, a debutante, encounters the harsh realities of her later life, including a loveless marriage and the crib death of her child.

But Burnett rejected many of his other short stories, and some of them were also spurned by *The Saturday Evening Post*, *Esquire*, *Collier's*, or the other magazines known as "slicks" because of their glossy paper that so appealed to advertisers. Salinger, realizing that he had to devote himself to his craft, quit school. One early story, "Go See Eddie," is a bleak tale in which a brother confronts his sister about an affair she's having with a married man. After making the rounds, the story did get published in late 1940, but only in an obscure academic journal published by the University of Kansas. And so it went, rejection after rejection.

Finally, in July 1941, *Collier's* printed "The Hang of It," a slight story about a soldier, training for war in 1917, who can't seem to get the hang of anything his sergeant is trying to drill into him. Salinger was said to be embarrassed by it.[32] That story was followed two months later by "The Heart of a Broken Story," a boy-meets-girl parody published in *Esquire*. Salinger narrates the story himself, boldly poking fun at the slick magazines that published his early work. He again shows his gift for dialogue, this time in the form of imagined letters between the boy and girl, who never do meet. It's funny, a rare feat for Salinger.

Salinger was on his way as a writer. In 1944, while at war in Europe, he sent Burnett a donation of $200, money he earned from the "slicks," to support a writing prize for college students (which Norman Mailer had won in 1941).[33] It was his way of saying thanks to his Columbia mentor and friend.

● ● ●

Despite his largess, Salinger's relationship with Burnett did not end well. *Story* published only two more Salinger stories, neither among his best: "Once a Week Won't Kill You," a war story published in the

November–December 1944 issue, and "Elaine," about a beautiful but intellectually challenged young woman who encounters her first love. It was published in the March–April 1945 issue. Burnett did offer to publish a collection of Salinger's short stories in Story Press, the magazine's book publishing imprint. But Story Press's partner, the Lippincott Company, vetoed the idea, and Burnett had to break the news to Salinger, who blamed Burnett. The two men didn't speak again for years.[34]

Burnett had another student in his writing class at Columbia: Hallie Southgate Abbett, whose work also appeared in *Story* magazine. She and Burnett became romantically involved, and soon thereafter Burnett divorced Martha Foley and married Hallie Abbett. (Foley went on to become the long-term editor of *Best American Short Stories*, an annual anthology that helped the careers of another crop of up-and-coming writers, including Saul Bellow, Bernard Malamud, Delmore Schwartz, Thomas Pynchon, and Joyce Carol Oates.)

Meanwhile, Whit Burnett tried to reconcile with Salinger, but Salinger, still blaming him for the Lippincott rejection, never responded to any of Burnett's overtures. Then, in 1964, twenty years later, Hallie Burnett wrote to Salinger asking him to contribute an introduction to a book celebrating *Story* magazine's thirty-third anniversary.[35] Remarkably enough, Salinger agreed, but this time it was Whit Burnett who rejected the peace offering, claiming Salinger's laudatory introduction was too much about Burnett and his class and not enough about *Story* magazine.

Whit Burnett died of a heart attack in 1973. At the time, Hallie Burnett was producing a book called *Fiction Writer's Handbook*, and she asked Salinger if she could publish Salinger's 1964 introduction as an epilogue to the book—the very piece Whit Burnett had rejected. Salinger agreed, and the salutation ran, entitled simply "A Salute to Whit Burnett." Here it is, slightly abbreviated:[36]

> *Back in 1939, when I was twenty, I was a student for a time in...Whit Burnett's short-story course, up at Columbia. A good and instructive and profitable year for me, on all counts, let me briefly say. Mr. Burnett simply and very knowledge-ably conducted a short-story course, never mugwumped over one. Whatever personal reasons he may have had for being there, at all, he plainly had no intentions of using fiction, short or long, as a leg up for him-self in the academic or quarterly-magazine hierarchies. He usually showed up for class late, praises on him, and contrived to slip out early—I often have my doubts whether any good and conscientious short-story-course conductor can humanly do more. Except that Mr. Burnett did. I have several*

notions how or why he did, but it seems essential only to say that he had a passion for good short fiction, strong short fiction, that very easily and properly dominated the room..."

...In class one evening, Mr. Burnett felt himself in the mood to read Faulkner's "The Evening Sun Go Down" out loud, and he went right ahead and did it...He abstained from reading beautifully... You got your Faulkner straight without any middlemen between... Regretfully, I never got to meet Faulkner, but I often had it in my head to shoot him a letter telling him about that unique reading of Mr. Burnett's...I wanted to tell Faulkner... that not once, throughout the reading, did Burnett come between the author and his beloved silent reader. Whether he has ever done it again, I don't know, but with somebody who has brought the thing off even once, the written short-story form must be very much at home, intact, unfinagled with, suitably content.

Salutes to Whit Burnett, to Hallie Burnett, and to all STORY readers and contributors.

J.D.S.

By citing Burnett's reading of Faulkner, Salinger was, I think, acknowledging the message he learned from his former mentor: that nothing should interfere with the relationship between the "silent reader" and the characters in the story he is reading. That, in turn, led Salinger to believe he should even withhold information that might guide readers to the author's own interpretation of a story's "meaning." If the ending of a Salinger story was ambiguous, and it often was, so be it. Let the readers draw their own conclusions.

Salinger's belated tribute to Burnett, published three years after Burnett died, was very much a heartfelt recognition of the debt he owed to his early teacher and mentor, perhaps even an apology for severing their friendship over a relatively trivial disagreement. It was a rare thing to see: Salinger as a mensch.

CHAPTER 3

Salinger at War

It was one thing to be published in *Story* magazine, or even such "slicks" as *Esquire, Collier's,* or *The Saturday Evening Post.* It was quite another to land a short story in *The New Yorker,* the *ne plus ultra* of magazines. And that was Salinger's goal, even if it meant enduring numerous rejections.

In October 1941, *The New Yorker* did accept a story aptly called "Am I Banging My Head Against the Wall?" Salinger described it in a letter that month to his good friend Elizabeth Murray as "a sad little comedy about a prep schoolboy on Christmas vacation."[37] The boy's name: Holden Caulfield. It was the first Salinger story that used Holden's name, leading a decade later to his star turn in *The Catcher in the Rye.*

Just days before the story was scheduled to be published in *The New Yorker,* the Japanese bombed Pearl Harbor on December 7, and the editors suspended the story indefinitely. In the face of war, who wanted to read a story about a prep school dropout who whines a lot?

•••

Even before Pearl Harbor, Salinger had sought to join the peacetime army, thinking it would bring structure to his life while he continued writing. But his attempt to enlist earlier in 1941 was turned down because of a mild heart irregularity. In a letter to Whit Burnett after his rejection, he complained with bitterness that he was "classified 1-B with all the other cripples and faggets."[38] The army later relaxed its standards, drafting him in April 1942. Private Salinger reported for duty at Fort Dix, New Jersey, on April 27, 1942.

He soon became an itinerant soldier, transferred from base to base, including stops in Bainbridge, Georgia; Nashville, Tennessee; and Fairfield, Ohio. Yet he managed to do some writing along the way. In Nashville, where he drafted press releases for the army's public information office, he used his three-day passes to register at a local hotel to work on his own writing. And in Fairfield, he sold three of his short stories about army life to *The Saturday Evening Post*, which were later published in a five-month burst in early 1944.[39]

One of the stories, "Last Day of the Last Furlough," introduced the character of Babe Gladwaller, a Salinger clone, who had the same army dog tag number as Salinger, the same sort of adoring mother, the same love of F. Scott Fitzgerald. In several stories featuring Gladwaller, Salinger was able to convey many of his own feelings about the war, especially his anger at what he saw as inept planning by army brass that resulted in unnecessary carnage to American GIs.

While he kept writing, Private Salinger applied for Officer Candidate School but was rejected. Instead, after some eighteen months in the army, he was accepted into the Counter Intelligence Corps and promoted to staff sergeant. Not a frontline soldier, he would be embedded in an army unit overseas, assigned to question German POWs and arrest any Nazi spies found in the local population. He was chosen for his unique role partly because he spoke German, a skill acquired during his ten-month stay in Vienna when he was an eighteen-year-old college dropout.

●●●

He shipped out to Europe in early 1944, stationed in Tiverton, in Devonshire, England. Then, on D-Day, June 6, 1944, Allied troops stormed the French beaches at Normandy, and Salinger was in the midst of combat. Assigned to the Twelfth Regiment of the Fourth Division, he landed at Utah Beach on the Normandy coast. He later told Whit Burnett that on D-Day he carried with him six chapters of a novel he was writing, which later became *The Catcher in the Rye*. Salinger thought of his pack of chapters as a lucky talisman, but he fully intended to work on the book even while on active duty in France.

Salinger was in the second wave of Allied soldiers at Normandy on D-Day, landing on Utah Beach soon after the first soldiers stormed ashore amid heavy German resistance at Omaha Beach, five miles away. Most of the Allied soldiers who died on D-Day were killed at Omaha Beach, but a few of Salinger's army buddies perished at Utah Beach.

In all, the D-Day landing was traumatic for Salinger, haunting him for many years, according to his daughter's memoir. She reports him saying more than once, "I landed on D-Day, you know, as if I understood the implications."[40] And those implications extended to the ten months of horror-filled war that Salinger endured after Normandy, influencing his fiction as well as his life.

In an unpublished story, "The Magic Foxhole," written later in 1944, Salinger described the Normandy landing, the only time he depicted the wrenching details of combat in his fiction. (The twenty-one-page typed manuscript is in the archives of *Story* magazine at the Princeton University Library.) The opening scene depicts a solitary soldier moving on a beach littered with the dead and wounded. He's the chaplain, frantically searching for his eyeglasses—until he, too, is gunned down. Critics have pointed out the symbolism of God's messenger finally being killed—the death of God—after searching for the clarity of battle that his eyeglasses might have provided.[41]

Nearly a year later, Salinger's view of God had changed. In "A Boy in France," published in *The*

Saturday Evening Post, (March 31, 1945), Salinger affirmed the existence of God, in effect, acknowledging his own spiritual quest. He did so through the fictional Babe Gladwaller, who imagined divine beauty in his young sister's innocence, just as Holden Caulfield would do in *The Catcher in the Rye*.

As Salinger's unit moved inland, joining the rest of the Twelfth Infantry Regiment, the men fought their way along the Normandy hedgerows and the French coastline toward the port city of Cherbourg—needed by the Allies to land soldiers, tanks, and supplies for the march to Germany. In and around Cherbourg, Salinger's regiment fought street by street, house by house while under German sniper fire. Of some 3,000 members of Salinger's regiment who had landed with him in Normandy on June 6, only 1,100 remained by the end of June. The rest were killed, wounded, or missing in action. It was the highest rate of casualties of any regiment in the entire war.[42]

Salinger wrote little about D-Day in his fiction and hardly anything at all in his letters home to Whit Burnett and others. But he did confess to Burnett his fear of war as the Allied troops advanced in France. In a letter dated June 28, 1944, he wrote:

> "I don't think I can write a pithy paragraph or two about the whole affair. I'm still scared. But I'll tell you this: you never saw six-feet-two of muscles and

typewriter ribbons get out of a Jeep and
into a ditch as fast as this baby can...No
use in being fool-hardy, I say."[43]

The only respite for Salinger's unit came when it marched into Paris along with other troops to liberate the French capital on August 25, 1944. It was a joyful time, with throngs of French citizens mobbing the Allied soldiers. Coming less than three months after the D-Day landings, the liberation of Paris was another historical moment for Salinger.

In another letter to Whit Burnett, on September 9, 1944, Salinger described the joy of the Parisians he encountered:

"They cried, they laughed, they kissed
us, they brought glasses of cognac up to
the Jeep, held their babies up for us for
kissing...If we had stood on top of the
Jeep and taken a leak, Paris would have
said, 'Ah, the darling Americans. What a
charming custom.'"[44]

In a moment of exuberance, Salinger decided to look for Ernest Hemingway, who was said to be in Paris as a war correspondent for *Collier's*. Salinger jumped into a Jeep with his army buddy John Keenan and headed straight to the Ritz Hotel. Where else would Hemingway be staying? Sure enough, there he was, the famed author of *The Sun Also Rises*, *A Farewell to*

Arms, and *For Whom the Bell Tolls.* The two writers—one a rookie, the other a legend—somehow bonded. They remained friends for years thereafter.[45]

In his letter to Burnett, Salinger described his meeting with Hemingway in Paris: "He's very soft; not at all big-shotty or patronizing, and he's modest without affectation." More important, Hemingway told him he liked Salinger's story that had just been published in The *Saturday Evening Post,* "Last Day of the Last Furlough." In the story, Salinger described wartime camaraderie in a conversation between two of his fictional characters, Babe Gladwaller and Vincent Caulfield, whose twenty-year-old brother was named Holden. As Vincent says to Babe:

> "GIs... belong together these days. It's no
> good being with civilians anymore. They
> don't know what we know, and we're no
> longer used to what they know. It doesn't
> work out so hot."

Such sentiments would have appealed to Hemingway. And the forty-five-year-old Hemingway did indeed take a shine toward Salinger, who was twenty years younger. "Jesus, he has a helluva talent," Hemingway said soon after.[46]

It was an ironic outcome since Salinger was no fan of Hemingway's fiction, much preferring the work of his idol, F. Scott Fitzgerald. In "Zooey," Salinger has

Buddy Glass, his alter ego, describe Fitzgerald's *The Great Gatsby* as his *Tom Sawyer*. In a letter to Elizabeth Murray, Salinger said he "hates" Hemingway's emphasis on physical courage, "commonly called guts. Probably because I'm short on it myself."[47] Their friendship even survived Holden Caulfield's critique in *The Catcher in the Rye* of Hemingway's *A Farewell to Arms*. Holden called it a "phony" book, just about the worst epithet in Holden's vocabulary.

Despite the privations of war, Salinger managed to find the time, space, and safety to do some writing of his own, often "under the most adverse conditions," recalled Keenan, his brother-in-arms and lifelong friend. "He would scribble on his writing pad or peck away at his portable typewriter, which he kept hidden in our Jeep."[48]

Salinger and Keenan grew close to two other members of the Counter Intelligence Corps, Paul Fitzgerald and Jack Altaras. Calling themselves "The Four Musketeers," they hung out together as much as possible and remained friends for decades to come. Paul Fitzgerald and Salinger corresponded regularly for sixty-five years after the war,[49] and Fitzgerald's war-time diary included Salinger's home address on Park Avenue, as well as his home phone number: Sacramento 2-7544.[50]

• • •

After some R&R in Paris, Salinger's unit faced months of relentless fighting with high casualties from artillery fire, landmines, and freezing conditions during the worst winter in memory. Many GIs who didn't have warm-enough coats or waterproof boots froze to death. In a particularly bloody battle in the Hurtgen Forest on Germany's border with Belgium and Luxembourg, Salinger's Fourth Infantry Division gained only three miles of wooded terrain in ten days of fighting but lost a thousand men per mile. Salinger survived, largely because Counter Intelligence officers weren't frontline soldiers, but he witnessed much of the horror. "They called it the meat factory, because it ground up so many Americans," said Alex Kershaw, the author of three books on World War II. "Salinger saw the futility and horror of that immense loss of life."[51]

Salinger himself wrote about Hurtgen Forest in a short story, "The Stranger," published by *Collier's* magazine in its issue dated December 1, 1945. In one passage he described the death of Vincent Caulfield. As Babe Gladwaller reports:

> "He [Vincent] and four other GIs and I were standing around a fire we made in Hurtgen Forest. Some mortar dropped in suddenly—it doesn't whistle or anything—and it hit Vincent and three of the other men. He died... not more than about three minutes after he was hit... I

think he had too much pain in too large
an area of his body to have realized anything but blackness...His eyes were open.
I think he recognized me and heard me
when I spoke to him, but he didn't say
anything at all."

Soon after Hurtgen Forest, Salinger's unit fought an
epic battle in Luxembourg, just across the Sauer River
from Germany. Called the Battle of the Bulge, it was
Hitler's last-gasp offensive, and by the time it ended,
in January 1945, it was said to be the greatest loss of
life in American military history. "It was so cold that
trucks had to be run every half hour or the oil in them
would freeze," reported Alex Kershaw, the war historian. "GIs took to urinating on their weapons to thaw
them out."[52]

Victorious American troops, who soon marched
through the area into Germany, discovered corpses of
thousands of their fellow GIs, "many with arms fro-
zen skyward, as if in supplication," wrote Kenneth
Slawenski, a Salinger biographer.[53]

Salinger occasionally spoke about his war experiences with his daughter, Margaret (known as Peggy),
and son, Matt. He explained how his nose got bent
when he jumped out of a Jeep under sniper fire, and
how he got deaf in one ear from a mortar shell that
exploded near him.[54] He spoke touchingly of his buddies in the army, especially Keenan, who became a New

York City police lieutenant (leading the "Son of Sam" mass-murder investigation). Salinger, then fifty-nine, even turned up to speak at Keenan's NYPD retirement party years in 1978 in New York's outer borough of Queens. "He was a great comfort," Salinger said of Keenan, especially "in the foxholes...In Normandy he led us all in song." It was a rare public appearance for Salinger, testimony of his affection for Keenan.[55]

He showed Peggy and Matt his army watch, his water canteen, and the medals he won. Once, Peggy reports, when her mother suggested an outdoor camping trip, Salinger snapped at her: "For Christ sake, Claire, I spent most of the war in foxholes. I will *never* spend another night outdoors if I can help it, I promise you."[56]

• • •

Perhaps Salinger's most devastating wartime experience occurred when his Fourth Infantry Division liberated several Nazi concentration camps. On April 27, 1945, just days before the war in Europe officially ended on May 8, American soldiers discovered a place called Kaufering Lager IV, one of eleven slave labor camps that were satellites of the concentration camp at Dachau, about forty-five miles away. Salinger's unit arrived the next day, and he was an eyewitness to the horrors the fleeing Nazis left behind, including the charred bodies of Jews too sick to leave who were simply burned to death in their barracks. Elsewhere lay the bodies of emaciated Jews who had starved to death or been shot by the Nazis. It was a traumatic experience for Salinger and many other GIs.

Peggy later said that her father told her, "You never really get the smell of burning flesh out of your nose entirely, no matter how long you live."[57]

After the fighting ended, Salinger was assigned to an outpost near Nuremberg. It didn't go well. He sank into a profound depression, a combination of combat shock, battle fatigue, and survivor guilt that today we would call post-traumatic stress disorder (PTSD). Salinger himself called it a nervous breakdown.[58]

Did Jewish GIs react differently to what they found in liberated concentration camps? Did Salinger? We have no way of knowing whether Salinger's Jewish heritage contributed to his subsequent breakdown. But it's worth noting that his collapse did not follow the catastrophic fighting he encountered in the Hurtgen Forest or during the Battle of the Bulge. It struck him soon after his unit liberated a concentration camp whose victims were nearly all Jews. "Kaufering Lager IV was what broke Salinger," said Eberhard Alsen, a literary critic who wrote of Salinger's wartime experience.[59]

Salinger rarely mentioned this trauma. His only known reference to a concentration camp came in the story "A Girl I Knew" that described the death, in Buchenwald, of the Jewish girl he knew in Vienna. (See page 16.)

In a letter to Elizabeth Murray on May 13, 1945, he referred obliquely to his "own little war over here." He said he had celebrated Germany's surrender by "wondering what close relatives would think if I fired a .45 slug neatly but effectively through the palm of my left hand and how long it would take me to learn to type with what was left of my hand."[60]

Clearly, something was wrong. But it wasn't until July 1945 that he sought help at the psychiatric clinic of a civilian hospital in Nuremberg, where he stayed for two weeks. He deliberately avoided a military hospital, hoping to escape the stigma of a psychiatric discharge from the army. Salinger decided to write Hemingway about his hospitalization, perhaps because he knew Hemingway had been wounded in 1917 in the Great War. In his "Dear Poppa" letter to Hemingway, he explained that "I've been in an almost constant state of despondency and I thought it would be good to talk to somebody sane."[61]

•••

Partly because he found it therapeutic, Salinger resumed writing short stories, including "The Stranger," his tale of the fighting in Hurtgen Forest. He later wrote of similar cases of war-caused depression in two of his most famous *New Yorker* short stories, "A Perfect Day for Bananafish" (January 31, 1948), which essentially launched his post-war eminence, and "For Esmé—with

Love and Squalor" (April 8, 1950), which the *New York Times* book critic Charles Poore hailed as "the best short story to have emerged from World War II."[62] Both stories were reprinted in Salinger's second book, *Nine Stories* in 1953. (See chapter 9.)

In "Bananafish" we encounter Seymour Glass, who, like Salinger, was an ex-sergeant in the army whose father was Jewish but whose mother was not. He, too, suffered a nervous breakdown at the end of the war, but, unlike Salinger, Seymour commits suicide.

"Esmé" introduces Sergeant X, who, again like Salinger, stormed the Normandy beach on D-Day and was hospitalized in Germany after he also had a nervous breakdown. Even after he is released, he still feels "his mind dislodge itself and teeter, like insecure luggage on an overhead rack." His hands shake so much that his handwriting is "almost entirely illegible." When Salinger's daughter later read through his wartime letters, she saw that the handwriting in his 1945 missives had become "something totally unrecognizable."[63]

Though Salinger was able to write short stories about the war, especially about battle-scarred protagonists, he blanched at the idea of writing a war novel:

> "So far, the novels of this war have had too much of the strength, maturity and craftsmanship critics are looking for, and too little of the glorious imperfections which teeter and fall off the best

minds. The men who have been in this war deserve some sort of trembling melody rendered without embarrassment or regret. I'll watch out for that book."[64]

Salinger's "trembling melody" arrived in his 1950 story, "For Esmé—With Love and Squalor." It was his touching tribute to his fellow soldiers, combined with a paean to the glorious innocence of a young girl.

Yet not even Sergeant X expresses any anger at the Nazis. Instead, he conveys Salinger's contempt for the war, especially the high command of the US military. These are familiar themes in Salinger's fiction and in many of his letters to friends. In "Last Day of the Last Furlough," he has Babe Gladwaller express his anger at how war is glamorized:

> "...it's the moral duty of all the men who have fought...in this war to keep our mouths shut, once it's over, never again to mention it in any way. It's time we let the dead die in vain... If we come back... making movies of heroism...the future generations will always be doomed to future Hitlers...If German boys had learned to be contemptuous of violence, Hitler would have had to take up knitting to keep his ego warm."

That remarkable warning against glorifying war was written well before D-Day, before Staff Sergeant Salinger had experienced even a single day of combat.

CHAPTER 4

The German Connection

By all accounts, Salinger was a dedicated soldier who ultimately won five battle stars and a citation for valor. But he hated the army's military command, blaming them for errors committed in the fog of war. In his letter to Elizabeth Murray on May 13, 1945, Salinger confessed that his hostility toward the army was "edgy with treason."[65]

He even told Hemingway of his misgivings about the war and his anger at the massive loss of life. In a letter Hemingway wrote to literary critic Malcolm Cowley on September 3, 1945, he said, "We had a kid named Jerry Slasinger—no Salinger—in one of the CIC teams in the division," adding that Salinger "wanted to be a writer and wrote well." But, Hemingway reported, he "hated the army and the war."[66]

And in *The Catcher in the Rye*, Salinger writes about Holden Caulfield watching a war movie about a wounded English soldier who loses his memory and doesn't even remember who he was. After the movie, Holden reflects, "I don't think I could stand it if I had to go to war...My brother D. B. was in the Army for four goddam years...he landed on D-Day and all—but I really think he hated the Army worse than the war... He said the Army was practically as full of bastards as the Nazis were."

At first, Salinger admired the US military's war effort, and he toed the line against Nazi aggression. He was especially sympathetic and tender-hearted to ordinary GIs in his war-time stories written before D-Day, such as "Personal Notes on an Infantryman" (1942) and "Soft-Boiled Sergeant" (1944). In "Soft-Boiled Sergeant," for instance, a GI named Philly Burns tells his wife, "I met more good guys in the Army than I ever knowed when I was a civilian."

And Babe Gladwaller remembers:

"The music of the unrecoverable years...
the pretty good years when all the dead
boys in the 12th Regiment had been living
and cutting in on all the other dead boys
on the dance floor...the years when no
one who could dance worth a damn had
ever heard of Cherbourg, or Saint-Lo, or
Hurtgen Forest, or Luxembourg."

In later stories, Salinger took a dimmer view of the war and the toll it exacted. In "A Boy in France," the tone is especially bleak, full of anguish and despair, with one American GI—again Babe Gladwaller—hallucinating in a foxhole next to a dead German soldier. He is muttering a line in a letter from Mattie, his younger sister: "Please come home soon."

Yet Salinger rarely, if ever, blamed the Nazis. In fact, he rarely used the word Nazi, the common epithet used by every GI. Instead, he called them Germans, Krauts, or just the enemy. He even had some of his characters express sympathy for German soldiers, including Sergeant X, the war-damaged American GI in "For Esmé—with Love and Squalor," his most famous short story. (See page 69.)

What changed Salinger's view so much? Mostly it was the carnage, which he viewed as unnecessary, the result of inept planning and execution.

In training for the D-Day invasion, for example, the army conducted a simulated attack in Slapton Sands, England. Salinger's unit participated, and it turned into a disaster. More than one hundred allied soldiers were killed by friendly fire from a British war ship. Another six hundred were killed by German torpedo boats that sank two Allied landing ships and crippled a third. Salinger and others in his Counter Intelligence unit barely avoided death, and they blamed the army brass.[67] Fair enough.

Later, at Hurtgen Forest, Salinger witnessed some of the worst casualties of the war, almost getting killed himself. And for what? The fighting at Hurtgen Forest was pretty much a stalemate, accomplishing little or nothing. Even many military leaders called it the wrong fight, in the wrong place, at the wrong time.[68] Again, fair enough. But Salinger rarely wrote about the battle, and when he did, as in "The Stranger" he never mentioned the Nazis or even Germany.

Judging from Salinger's later fiction about the war and his letters to friends, the enemy men fighting for Hitler were just soldiers, no different from their American counterparts. At one point, said his army buddy John Keenan, Salinger even intervened to save a group of wounded German soldiers about to be killed by angry American GIs.[69]

According to Eberhard Alsen, the literary historian who wrote about Salinger's wartime experience, Salinger never invoked the war's larger purpose: the battle between totalitarianism and democracy, between dictatorship and freedom. He consistently ducked the opportunity to indict the Nazis for their crimes, Alsen wrote—or to acknowledge that the US Army brass he so disdained was actually up against an historic evil.[70]

But why? Salinger never offered a word of explanation in anything he published or said publicly. Clearly, Salinger had an affinity for Germans. He spoke their language. He lived in Germany for nearly a year after the war. He married a German woman. And he hated the American army brass. Somehow, as a result of all this, Salinger seemed to downplay Hitler's agenda, and even the horror of the Holocaust, which he had personally witnessed at a liberated concentration camp.

I still find it something of a mystery.

CHAPTER 5

Jerry and His War Bride

Though Salinger could have returned to the US after the war ended, he signed up for another stint with the Counter Intelligence Corps. He chose to stay in Germany largely because he had met a German woman named Sylvia Welter. According to the rumor mill, Sylvia was a low-level Nazi party official or perhaps an informer for the Gestapo, the Nazi secret police, and Salinger is said to have arrested her as part of his duties to ferret out Nazi sympathizers. Even Salinger's daughter, Peggy, wrote in her 2000 memoir that she believed that, at the very least, Sylvia was a Jew-hating Nazi sympathizer.

The truth, however, seems quite different. Eberhard Alsen, the American academic, who was born in Germany, dug into German archives, publishing an academic study in 2018 called *J. D. Salinger and the Nazis*. His book is tough on Salinger in many ways, but it does conclude that Welter was not a member of the Nazi Party.

Here's Alsen's story of how their relationship started:[71]

> Sylvia Luise Welter was born in Frankfurt on April 19, 1919. Her birth certificate lists her nationality as German, and the records show she received her medical degree from the University of Innsbruck on February 6, 1945. According to Alsen's research, Welter met Salinger in May 1945, less than a month after the war ended. Five months later, on October 18, 1945, Jerry and Sylvia were married.
>
> Because it was illegal under military rules for an American soldier to marry a German, Sylvia passed herself off as French, aided and abetted by Salinger, who forged a French passport for her. He was able to do so because one of his tasks as a Counter Intelligence agent was to issue new identification papers for thousands of foreign nationals who had been displaced by the war. The erroneous notion that Sylvia was French persisted for years. As late as 1988, Ian Hamilton twice referred to Sylvia as French in his otherwise revealing book, *In Search of J. D. Salinger.*[72]

Salinger was formally discharged from the army in November 1945, but he signed up as a civilian for a six-month stint to assist in the Allied occupation of Germany and its "de-Nazification." He also bought a dog, a black Schnauzer he named Benny. In May 1946, after his post-war duties were over, the Salinger couple, along with Benny, sailed to New York aboard a naval ship, the USS *Ethan Allen.* Sylvia still claimed French citizenship.[73]

For some hard-to-fathom reason, Jerry decided to move with Sylvia into his parents' Park Avenue apartment. The arrangement, predictably enough, was a disaster. Salinger's parents quickly figured out that Sylvia was German, and after a month or so of strife with Salinger's mother, Sylvia awoke one morning to find an airplane ticket to Germany waiting for her on the breakfast table.[74] She promptly moved back to Germany.

In the eight months that Sylvia and Jerry lived together as a married couple, he didn't write anything: no short stories, no work on his novel, and hardly any letters to friends. For a man who wrote nearly every day, even in wartime, it was an extraordinary departure from the norm.

Alsen's research did reveal "something strange" about Sylvia's earlier life in Germany. It turned out that Sylvia had enrolled at six different universities on her way to earning a medical degree. Why? "Could it be possible," Alsen asks, "that the Gestapo enrolled Sylvia in six universities to spy on anti-Nazi student organizations?" Then Alsen answers his own question: "...there is no documentary proof that she had anything to do with the Gestapo."[75]

Did Salinger, a wartime intelligence agent, know of these rumors? Did he learn about it after he and Sylvia came to New York? Did it contribute to the breakup of his marriage? We don't know.

In any case, it wasn't until January 26, 1949, nearly three years later, that Salinger had the marriage formally annulled in New York. It isn't clear why he waited so long. A few years later, Sylvia mailed a letter to Salinger, but he ripped it up without opening it, according to Salinger's daughter Peggy.[76] Sylvia eventually married another American and moved to North Carolina, where she set up an ophthalmology practice, still claiming to be French. She died on July 16, 2007, in Henderson, North Carolina.[77]

Even if Salinger did not believe the rumors about Sylvia, or even know of them, what was he thinking at the time? Why would a man raised Jewish, who was traumatized by the war and by what he saw of the Holocaust in a liberated concentration camp, think it would be okay to bring his German wife into his Jewish father's home right after the war?

Perhaps, as Alsen theorizes, it was all part of Salinger's denial mechanism for coping with his trauma: to deliberately close his eyes to the horror around him. Or, I'd venture to say, maybe it was his denial of all things Jewish in his life. After all, Salinger was a man who played down his own Jewishness before the war, who had no interest in pursuing Jewish themes in his fiction, and who rarely even mentioned what he saw in a concentration camp at war's end.

In sum, Alsen writes, Salinger "did not identify with the six million Jews the Nazis murdered." He didn't deny the Holocaust, says Alsen, but "he definitely tried to ignore it."[78]

CHAPTER 6

"Tall, Dark, and Handsome"

A strange thing happened to Salinger after Sylvia returned to Germany in May 1946: He became quite the man about town. And he did so while still living in his parents' Park Avenue apartment and writing during the day. Most nights, though, he went clubbing, usually to Greenwich Village, an emerging hot spot for young writers and actors. He frequented nightclubs such as the Blue Angel, dined at restaurants such as Renato's, and drank at Chumley's, a hangout that mounted photos of its regular literary luminaries on its dreary walls. (Some years later, Chumley's hung Salinger's photograph, right next to that of one of his favorite writers, Ring Lardner.)[79]

Salinger began dating a string of young women, often bringing them to the various clubs and restaurants he frequented in Greenwich Village. Some of his dates remembered that he was eager to give them reading lists on Zen Buddhism, which he had begun to study. Later, after *The Catcher in the Rye* was published, some women recalled that he talked about his fictional characters as if they were real people: "Holden wouldn't like this or Phoebe didn't want to do that."[80]

He was routinely described as "tall, dark, and handsome," an apt image: He was six feet two inches tall, had near-black hair and eyes, and, judging from photographs at the time, I'd agree he was a good-looking guy. He evidently cared how he looked: he worked out with barbells to build up his scrawny frame. And he made an impression on the women he met, especially after *Catcher* was published in 1951.

One woman, the wife of a New York editor, met Salinger at a book party. "I was not prepared for the extraordinary impact of his physical presence," she recalled. "There was a kind of black aura about him. He was dressed in black; he had black hair, dark eyes, and he was of course extremely tall. I was kind of spellbound."[81]

Leila Hadley, a travel writer who briefly dated Salinger, had a very similar reaction. "He never talked about himself and he resented any personal questions about his family or his background...But he did have this extraordinary presence, very tall with a sort of darkness surrounding him. His face was like an El Greco. It wasn't a sexual power, it was a mental power...It was as if one's mind were at risk, rather than one's virtue."[82]

● ● ●

Don Congdon, a fiction editor at *Collier's*, lived on Charlton Street, near the heart of the action, and he invited Salinger to join his weekly poker game. "He was a lousy poker player," recalled A. E. Hotchner, a writer and editor who was a member of the group. "He refused to bluff,"[83] possibly because he deemed it phony.

Afterwards, Hotchner and Salinger often went to Chumley's. As Hotchner told it, Salinger was dismissive of many writers, including Hemingway. He even criticized Hotchner himself because his stories didn't connect to his life: "There's no hidden emotion in these stories," Salinger told Hotchner, "no fire between the words." Hotchner readily agreed. "He was right, of course."[84]

Yet Salinger was arrogant about his own writing and convinced of his literary destiny. He had "an ego of cast iron," Hotchner later said.[85] Salinger's pretentious claims gained some credibility after *The New Yorker* published "Slight Rebellion off Madison" in December 1946.

Because Salinger liked jazz, he and Hotchner often went to jazz clubs, such as the Blue Angel, where he especially admired Billie Holiday. "He was a different kind of person when he was enjoying the talent of a singer," said Hotchner. "These were the best of times with Jerry because he was the most natural."[86]

Hotchner and Salinger eventually had a falling out. In 1948, Hotchner was an editor at *Cosmopolitan*, one of the "slick" magazines that had regularly published Salinger stories. After one poker game in Greenwich Village, Salinger mentioned to Hotchner that he was planning to submit a story to *Cosmopolitan* called "Scratchy Needle on a Phonograph Record," which was based on the death of Bessie Smith, a blues singer much admired by Salinger. Hotchner was enthusiastic. He remembers Salinger saying that not one word of the story could be changed.

And not one word was changed. But unbeknownst to Hotchner, the title was re-written at the last minute to "Blue Melody." Hotchner called Salinger:

> "Listen, I gotta see you," Hotchner recalled saying. "Can we have a beer at Chumley's tonight?"

They met, and Hotchner explained what had happened, handing Salinger the magazine. Salinger exploded. "He said it was a terrible deceit on my part. I had promised. He was furious about it. And he walked out...He left me with my beer, sitting at the table. He took the magazine with him. I never saw him again."[87]

"Blue Melody" turned out to be one of the only Salinger stories that dealt explicitly with social problems in America. The story was an ode to Bessie Smith, the famous blues singer who died in an auto accident in

1937. She bled to death, it was rumored, after a hospital allegedly denied her admission because she was black. Salinger used the incident to take on America's racism toward its own black citizens. In effect, Salinger was asking, "Is this what we fought for against the Nazis?"

When Salinger turned twenty-eight in January 1947, he finally moved out of his parents' apartment, renting a loft in Tarrytown, New York, a suburb just north of the city. In a letter the following August to Elizabeth Murray, he called it "a little made-over garage which my landlady rather irritatingly calls the studio." But his Tarrytown digs proved too small, and Salinger moved several months later to a small house in Stamford, Connecticut, owned by Himan Brown, a successful producer of radio shows, especially such mysteries as *Inner Sanctum*, *The Adventures of the Thin Man*, and *Bulldog Drummond*. Brown almost turned down Salinger as a tenant because he insisted on bringing along Benny, his black Schnauzer, but Brown relented.[88]

In October 1949, Salinger moved again, with Benny, this time from Stamford to Westport, the same Connecticut town in which F. Scott Fitzgerald started writing *The Beautiful and Damned* in 1920. There, Salinger finished "For Esmé—with Love and Squalor," the only story he published between April 1949 and July 1951. And there he wrote the final version of *The Catcher in the Rye*.

In all, his years in suburbia proved fruitful. One theory holds that the conformity of suburban life in the late 1940s and early 1950s gave Salinger ample material to take on the ego-driven materialism he despised, as well as Holden Caulfield's "phonies." Salinger never said so, of course, but his fiction of the time was probing the very nature of human behavior.

"The Inverted Forest," for instance, was a thirty-thousand-word novella that explored the conflict between the material, social world of everyday life and the spiritual, creative world of imaginative life. The story is not quite successful, I think, in depicting Salinger's emerging views that art is inherently spiritual. But the story did presage Salinger's view that the artist needed to cloister himself away from the distraction and temptations of modern life.

"The Inverted Forest" was published in the December 1947 issue of *Cosmopolitan,* a month before *The New Yorker* published the far-superior story "A Perfect Day for Bananafish." In a sense, "The Inverted Forest" marked the end of Salinger's apprenticeship, while "Bananafish" represented his breakthrough to literary greatness. (See page 65.) It's hard to believe both stories were written by the same author at about the same time.

Salinger finally ended his suburban retreat in the summer of 1951, moving back to New York City, where he rented a small apartment at 300 East 57th Street, near Sutton Place. Perhaps concerned all this was far too posh for a man professing simplicity and humility, Salinger furnished it sparsely and entirely in black, according to Leila Hadley.[89] Or perhaps the color black reflected his continuing depression, which was not ameliorated even by his growing success as a writer.

CHAPTER 7

Here at *The New Yorker*

On his own in post-war America, Salinger thought of little else but becoming a big-time writer for *The New Yorker*. He had tried before, starting in 1941, when he was twenty-two. The magazine rejected several of his early stories, some with intriguing titles such as "Men Without Hemingway," "I Went to School with Adolph Hitler," and "Monologue for a Watery Highball."[90] But now he had to make amends for a problem of his own making.

In January 1944, just before the army shipped him to Europe, Salinger had written to Wolcott Gibbs, a fiction editor at *The New Yorker*, saying that his agent would soon submit a new story, called "Elaine." Then, in a display of *chutzpah*, his letter turned astonishingly arrogant. Salinger all but demanded that not a single word in the story be changed. And for good measure Salinger suggested that the magazine push several regular contributors to produce better stories. Among his targets: John Cheever and John O'Hara.[91]

Think about it: at that point in his career, Salinger was little more than a promising short-story writer off at war in Europe, and *The New Yorker* had never published a Salinger story, rejecting many of them. A couple of weeks later, Salinger got the answer he didn't want but surely deserved: William Maxwell, a top editor at *The New Yorker*, responded quite succinctly to Dorothy Olding, Salinger's agent:

> "This J. D. Salinger just doesn't seem quite right for us."[92]

Toward the end of November 1946, Salinger learned to his surprise that *The New Yorker* would finally publish "Slight Rebellion off Madison," the story that had gotten delayed by the Pearl Harbor attack in 1941. Apparently, Salinger's behavior nearly three years earlier was forgiven as a miscue under wartime pressure, maybe even forgotten. With great excitement, he wrote to William Maxwell, expressing enthusiasm and gratitude. Perhaps by way of apology for the earlier exchange, Salinger volunteered that he would make any editorial changes the magazine requested. The story, considerably revised, ran in the issue dated December 21, 1946, the first of many Salinger stories published by *The New Yorker*.

"Slight Rebellion off Madison" was originally called "Am I Banging My Head Against the Wall?" and was, in its earlier and unpublished version, Salinger's first story to use Holden Caulfield as a protagonist. Holden, a student at Pencey Prep, arranges to meet Sally Hayes on a Christmas-week break in New York. They see a Broadway show and go ice skating at the Radio City Rink. Holden, unhappy at school, then proposes that they run away together to a house in Vermont or Massachusetts. Sally, sensible girl that she is, dismisses the idea. Later, Holden drunkenly calls Sally twice on a payphone. They talk briefly the first time, and she never answers the second call. Holden, tears in his eyes, walks to the bus stop. The story ends with Holden waiting for a bus on Madison Avenue. "It was," writes Salinger, "a long wait."

Salinger later adapted the story as chapter 17 in *The Catcher in the Rye*. But he wisely changed the magazine story, which was narrated in the third person, to a much more intimate first-person account narrated by Holden in the book. The reader thus learns Holden's thoughts and feelings in a profoundly more emotional way.[93]

Encouraged by his success at *The New Yorker*, Salinger submitted a new story called "The Bananafish." William Maxwell responded to Salinger's agent:

> "We like part of 'The Bananafish,' by J. D. Salinger very much, but it seems to us to lack any discoverable story or point. If Mr. Salinger is around town, perhaps he'd like to come in and talk to me about *New Yorker* stories."[94]

Soon Salinger agreed with Maxwell that the story needed major revision, and he set about doing it. When he resubmitted it to Gus Lobrano, who was assigned to edit it, the story was returned to Salinger for yet more work. After a year back and forth, *The New Yorker* finally accepted "Bananafish," now renamed "A Fine Day for Bananafish." Among the many changes: Salinger added an opening section, a phone conversation between Muriel, Seymour Glass's wife, and her mother. In just ten pages, Salinger again deployed his gift for brilliant dialogue to define the characters and advance the narrative.

By the time of publication in the issue dated January 31, 1948, the story was renamed yet again: "A Perfect Day for Bananafish." When it came out, John Cheever, a regular contributor to *The New Yorker*, wrote to Lobrano, "I thought the Salinger piece was one hell of a story."[95] He was hardly alone. It "made a huge splash," said critic Ben Yagoda, who wrote a history of *The New Yorker*. "He became a sensation in the literary world."

There was, of course, no such creature called a bananafish. It was invented by Salinger's father, Sol, when he played in the ocean with Doris and Sonny as children. "Keep your eyes peeled for the bananafish," Doris later recalled their father telling them.[96] Naturally enough, the ever-scrupulous editors at *The New Yorker* asked whether *bananafish* should be spelled as one word or two. Salinger promptly said one word. And so it was.[97]

The story features Seymour Glass, the oldest of the seven Glass siblings. Like Salinger, Seymour is an army veteran suffering from psychological problems brought on by the war. He, too, had been hospitalized after the war. A cryptic story, "A Perfect Day for Bananafish" traces Seymour's encounter with a four-year-old girl, Sybil, on a Florida beach, telling her about a fantastic species of fish who die when they are trapped underwater by their own gluttony. They simply ate too many bananas. It ends with Seymour shooting himself to death in his hotel room, next to his wife, Muriel, who is lying in bed.

Some readers saw the story as an allegory of the fate of a hypersensitive man in a materialistic world, the only sane man in a world gone mad.[98] Or, in another interpretation, Seymour, like the bananafish, is trapped by some personal impulse, having nothing to do with society's ills. Or it might have been "shell shock," or "combat fatigue," caused by Seymour's experience in the war, what we now call PTSD.

Or, in a Zen interpretation, Seymour identified with the innocence of the "enlightened" child, Sybil, who is open, spontaneous, and honest, while abhorring the ego-driven, materialistic world of adults—Muriel, in this case. In this view, "A Perfect Day for Bananafish" is Salinger's first sustained attempt to integrate Buddhist insights into his fiction. The Sybil/Muriel contrast thus becomes a vivid example of Seymour's existential dilemma, a quandary so untenable that it led to his suicide.

Whatever the interpretation, the story was an instant hit. Eager to retain Salinger at *The New Yorker*, Lobrano offered him a "first reading agreement" binding him to the magazine for an annual retainer, said to be $30,000 in the first year, a remarkable sum—equivalent to $347,000 today.[99] Under the terms of the deal, Salinger would first offer any story he wrote to *The New Yorker*. Only if rejected could he sell it elsewhere. It was a rare and lucrative honor, and Salinger, in a burst of creative energy, published three more stories in *The New Yorker* over the next fourteen months: "Uncle Wiggily in Connecticut," "Just Before the War with the Eskimos," and "The Laughing Man."

Lobrano was now a key figure in Salinger's writing life. His brilliance as an editor was a major reason for Salinger's breakthrough success in 1948. Five years later, a grateful Salinger dedicated *Nine Stories* to Lobrano (along with Salinger's agent, Dorothy Olding).

●●●

Lobrano had come to *The New Yorker* in 1937 at the behest of E. B. White, a writer at the magazine, who had been Lobrano's college roommate at Cornell University. White's wife, Katharine, was the magazine's fiction editor, and she helped groom Lobrano, as did William Maxwell, Lobrano's immediate superior. Lobrano tended to bond with his writers, often the "older brother" to younger writers, including Salinger.[100]

Trouble soon erupted. Maxwell, a novelist who had joined the magazine in 1934, expected to succeed Katharine White as fiction editor when the Whites moved to Maine. But when Maxwell returned from a few days away, he discovered Lobrano sitting in Katharine White's office—her successor as fiction editor. Maxwell quit the magazine, but Lobrano lured him back, and the two men became good friends until Lobrano's sudden death in 1956 at age fifty-three. Salinger stayed above the fray, becoming especially close to Maxwell, who outlived Lobrano by more than forty years.[101]

Though Salinger was firmly established as a regulator contributor, the magazine frequently rejected some of his stories. One story that Lobrano turned down in 1949 was entitled "The Boy in the People Shooting Hat." Even *The New Yorker*'s judgment was not infallible: Much of that story ended up in *The Catcher in the Rye*, comprising most of chapters three to seven.

●●●

Soon after, *The New Yorker* printed what was Salinger's most successful short story, possibly his most famous: "For Esmé—with Love and Squalor," which ran in its April 8, 1950, issue. The story deals, in a poignant and uplifting way, with Salinger's own wartime trauma, and he wrote it specifically as a tribute to the soldiers who served and suffered.

In the first part of the story, set in April 1944, an unnamed American sergeant, who is a writer, is sitting in an English tearoom by himself, much like Tiverton, the town where Salinger was stationed just before D-Day. The sergeant is lonely, depressed, and awaiting the Allied invasion of Nazi-occupied France, just two months away.

Nearby sits a young British girl named Esmé, thirteen or so, who is caring for her seven-year-old brother, Charles. Both have been orphaned in the war. In honor of her father, Esmé wears his large army watch. Sensing the sergeant's loneliness, she and Charles sit at the sergeant's table and start a conversation. When she tells of her father's death in the war, she spells out the word s-l-a-i-n, trying to spare Charles any further hurt. She is determined not to be bitter about what the war has done, but to retain compassion and protect her brother. As they leave the tearoom, Esmé promises to correspond with the sergeant.

In the second part of the story, the war is over, and the unnamed GI is now Sergeant X, trying to recover from a nervous breakdown in a house once owned by a German family. Sergeant X picks up a book written by Goebbels and reads the inscription on the book's flyleaf. Salinger writes:

"Written in ink, in German, in a small, hopelessly sincere handwriting, were the words, 'Dear God, life is hell.'...X stared at the page for several minutes, trying, against heavy odds, not to be taken in. Then, with far more zeal than he had done anything in several weeks, he picked up a pencil stub, and wrote down, under the inscription, in English, 'Fathers and teachers, I ponder What is Hell? I maintain that it is the suffering of being unable to love.' He started to write Dostoevsky's name under the inscription. But saw—with fright that ran through his whole body—that what he had written was almost entirely illegible. He shut the book."

Soon after, Sergeant X is saved by love. He receives a small package from Esmé containing the watch worn by her father before he was killed by the Nazis. Her note said she hoped "that you will use it to greater advantage in these difficult days than I ever can..." The watch, she says, is "waterproof and shockproof." The note ends with a P.S. from Charles: "HELLO HELLO HELLO...LOVE AND KISSES CHARLES."

Sergeant X is overcome with emotion, moved by Esmé's affection, her love for her brother, and her compassion in the face of overwhelming grief. He senses that love can also help him conquer his own trauma, and we the readers are assured that he will. It is a catharsis for Sergeant X, and perhaps for Salinger as well. It is a rare, upbeat ending for a Salinger story. And very powerful.

The watch is a significant symbol, as many critics have observed. At first, it symbolizes Esmé's connection with her dead father and the tragedy of war. Then, when Sergeant X discovers that the watch has stopped working, its crystal cracked, it symbolizes his own plight after his nervous breakdown. Yet he realizes that while the watch may be broken, it still shows the profound effects of love and compassion.[102]

As critic Dan Wakefield points out in a 1958 essay, the unspoiled love of children is found in much of Salinger's fiction.[103] But nowhere else does it provide such an explicit resolution of a problem—certainly not with the poignance expressed in "For Esmé—with Love and Squalor."

● ● ●

In 1951, when *The Catcher in the Rye* was nearing publication, Salinger understandably thought *The New Yorker* would be interested in publishing an excerpt from the novel. Much to his surprise, and astonishing in retrospect, *The New Yorker* said no. Lobrano wrote that he and another editor—probably Maxwell—didn't find the characters believable: "The notion that in one family [the Caulfields] there are four such extraordinary children...is not quite tenable."[104]

Lobrano went on to say that Salinger seemed "imprisoned" by the novel, meaning that *The Catcher in the Rye* violated *The New Yorker*'s credo that its fiction should emphasize the story and subordinate the writer. The novel, Lobrano said, fell victim to "writer-consciousness."[105] In other words, he implied, Salinger was showing off. *The New Yorker* finally changed its tune when Little, Brown and Company published *The Catcher in the Rye* on July 16, 1951. In a book review, the magazine said Salinger's novel was "brilliant, fun, and meaningful." In a long review, S. N. Behrman concluded, in Holden's voice: "I loved this novel. I mean it—I really did."[106]

●●●

Soon after the debut of *The Catcher in the Rye*, the entire *New Yorker* family, including Salinger, was shocked to learn that Harold Ross, the iconic founding editor of the magazine, was ill. It wasn't clear what was wrong, but in a sure sign that it was serious, Ross, fifty-nine, didn't show up at the office on many days. Ross had created *The New Yorker* with his wife, Jane Grant, in 1925 and presided over every issue in the twenty-five-plus years since then—1,399 issues in all.[107]

Salinger liked and respected Ross, and the two were friendly. Ross had even less formal education than

Salinger, having dropped out of school in Utah when he was thirteen. He learned a lot along the way: as an itinerant reporter at several small newspapers around the country, as a staffer for the *Stars and Stripes* in Paris during World War I, and as an editor at a couple of small magazines in New York. Ross enjoyed poking fun at his lack of a high school diploma by asking his *New Yorker* colleagues, "Was Moby Dick the man or the whale?"[108]

Salinger wrote to him, expressing concern and his hopes for a speedy recovery. He made plans to visit Ross in October but cancelled when he himself got sick. Ross wrote back, suggesting a re-scheduled meeting. "I'll put you down for next spring," he wrote.[109]

It never happened. Ross did manage to return to work, but not for long. With his condition worsening, he was hospitalized for exploratory surgery on December 6, 1951. The doctors discovered a large tumor in his right lung, and he died on the operating table. On December 10, Salinger attended the funeral service, along with the staff of the magazine, at the Frank E. Campbell Funeral Home in New York.[110]

It was clear nobody could replace Ross, but someone had to succeed him. Among the leading candidates was Lobrano, which pleased Salinger. Though Lobrano had often been the editor who had to break any bad news to Salinger about a story that needed considerable work ("Bananafish," for example) or a story that was rejected ("Down at the Dinghy," to name one of many),

Lobrano had learned to work well with the very touchy Salinger. They remained friendly, even after Lobrano declined to excerpt *The Catcher in the Rye*.[111]

But the magazine's owner, Raoul Fleischmann, had someone else in mind as Ross's successor. Fleischmann had launched *The New Yorker* with Ross and his wife in 1925, putting up much of the money and serving as proprietor since opening day. Based on a suggestion from Ross, Fleischmann selected a lesser-known editor, William Shawn, who had been on the magazine's staff since 1933. Lobrano "never forgave Shawn or anyone else," according to E.B. White.[112]

Shawn was almost the opposite of Ross: Where Ross was lively and outgoing, Shawn was shy and withdrawn. But he had a steely core: Shawn's first act as editor was to demolish Ross's office and move the new center of power to the opposite end of the floor.[113]

● ● ●

Shawn was born William Chon in 1907, but later changed his name because, he said, it sounded Asian. He came from a family of non-observant Jews in Chicago, where his father ran a prosperous cutlery business in the meat-packing district. He dropped out of the University of Michigan after his sophomore year, worked odd jobs around the country, got married, and moved to New York in 1932, where he landed an entry-level job at *The New Yorker*.

At *The New Yorker*, Shawn was full of various phobias and eccentricities. He always carried an umbrella, rain or shine. Even in the summer, he wore wool suits, sweaters, and overcoats. He ate lunch at the Algonquin hotel nearly every day, but rarely ordered anything but cornflakes. Two employees were stationed outside his office to prevent people from walking in unexpectedly.[114] And because he was so afraid of getting stuck in the elevator, *The New Yorker*'s office building reserved a manned elevator for Shawn's regular use.[115]

Like Salinger, Shawn was obsessed with privacy and secrecy. Yet he carried on a decades-long, very public affair with Lillian Ross, one of the magazine's star writers. All the while, Shawn lived at home with his wife and, for many years, with his children.

Much to Salinger's delight, Shawn had many of the instincts and skills that made him a great editor, including a gift for generating story ideas. He directed *The New Yorker*'s coverage during World War II, persuading Ross to devote an entire issue, dated August 23, 1946, to John Hersey's brilliant recreation of the atomic bombing of Hiroshima.

Shawn generally left the fiction editing to his senior staff. Lobrano was Salinger's editor, and Shawn didn't get much involved. The process worked smoothly when *The New Yorker* published "Franny" in 1955. It was a well-crafted story about the youngest Glass sibling, then a college student undergoing a spiritual crisis. There's more than a touch of religion in it, with Franny frequently invoking the Jesus prayer: "Lord Jesus Christ have mercy on me." And there's a mysterious ending that led to much discussion of the story's meaning. The story sailed through the editing process and drew rave notices from readers and scholars, further enhancing Salinger's reputation. Salinger made it clear that many other Glass stories would follow. (Chapter 11.)

• • •

Later that year, the magazine published "Raise High the Roofbeam, Carpenters," not beloved by editors at *The New Yorker*, but well received by readers. In the story, Salinger resurrected Seymour from "Bananafish" and united him with Franny, as brother and sister in the Glass family, a crew of seven precocious siblings. This time around, another brother, Buddy, who serves as Salinger's alter ego in the Glass stories, narrates his memory of Seymour's wedding in 1942, which Seymour neglects to attend. Salinger is clearly obsessed with Seymour as ghost and guru of Eastern mysticism, but he crafted a tale that is funny and touching, perhaps his last successful story in *The New Yorker*.

Things changed dramatically when "Zooey" came along two years later. By this time, Maxwell had taken over the never-easy task of dealing with Salinger after Lobrano died in 1956. Maxwell and Katharine White, now back from Maine, didn't like the story at all. They saw it as a long, meandering piece saturated with religion. Not mystical Christianity this time, as in "Franny," but rather with Zen Buddhism, Salinger's latest enthusiasm. The editors rejected the story, with Maxwell delivering the bad news to Salinger.[116]

Salinger was distraught, partly because the rejection upended his grand plans for more sequels about the Glass family. Then, out of the blue, he received a check from *The New Yorker* for "Zooey," as if the story had been accepted, not rejected. Unbeknown to Salinger, Shawn had overruled his editors and decided to publish the story. To complicate matters even more, Shawn decreed that he would edit "Zooey" himself, dealing directly with Salinger without any help from Maxwell or White.[117]

For the next six months, they closeted themselves in Shawn's office day after day, relentlessly revising "Zooey" word by word. In the process, the two men became close, devoted friends—to the point that when Salinger's daughter, Peggy, was born in 1955, Shawn became her godfather. "Zooey," a joint Salinger/Shawn production, was published with Salinger's byline in *The New Yorker* in the issue dated May 7, 1957. Similarly, Shawn was deeply involved when *The New Yorker* published "Seymour: An Introduction" in its June 6, 1957, issue.

•••

It's hard to overstate *The New Yorker*'s importance to Salinger. In all, he wrote thirteen stories for the magazine, including seven of the stories that later appeared in his second book, *Nine Stories*. And all four major Glass stories from *The New Yorker* appeared—years later—in Salinger's last two books: first *Franny and Zooey*, followed by *Raise High the Roof Beam, Carpenters and Seymour: An Introduction*. In effect, Salinger wrote only one original book, *The Catcher in the Rye*. His other three books were all reprints of short stories that first ran elsewhere, nearly all of them in *The New Yorker*. (See Appendix for a complete list of Salinger's published fiction.)

After Salinger had published all his books, he began work on a new story for *The New Yorker*, yet another piece on the Glass family, entitled "Hapworth 16, 1924." It ran to 28,000 words, more novella than short story, and was roundly scorned by editors at *The New Yorker*, who wanted to reject it flat out. Once again, Shawn overruled them, editing the piece himself. It was published in *The New Yorker*'s issue of June 19, 1965, taking up almost the entire issue.

"Hapworth" consists largely of a letter written by Seymour Glass to his family in 1924 from a camp in Hapworth, Maine, where Seymour, then seven, and his brother Buddy, then five, are spending the summer. Seymour is a boy genius, who writes poetry, speaks like a graduate student, and talks of Vedanta, an offshoot of Hinduism. Buddy, no slouch himself, writes short stories and proceeds to narrate Seymour's letter to the rest of us. There is much said of God and Jesus, of Vedanta and Zen, and of spirituality versus materialism—all reflecting Salinger's own religious quest. A complex and difficult story, "Hapworth" was the least readable of anything that Salinger ever published.

Years later, as word spread that Salinger was planning to turn "Hapworth" into a book, critics pounced. Nothing was more scathing than the broadside written by Michiko Kakutani in the *New York Times Book Review*, more than thirty years after the story initially ran in *The New Yorker*. Salinger's novella, she wrote, was a "sour, implausible, and, sad to say, completely charmless story."[118]

Kakutani also dismissed much of the entire Glass canon of stories as "elliptical" and "self-conscious." When she soon won a Pulitzer Prize for criticism, it was as if her negative review of "Hapworth" and of Salinger's Glass works received a ringing endorsement from the high priests of literature.

Salinger later dropped his plans to publish the story as a book, following the bad reviews, as well as a dispute with the potential publisher, an obscure one-man shop called Orchises Press in Arlington, Virginia.

Orchises Press was run by Roger Lathbury, a professor of English at George Mason University. He had written to Salinger in 1988 proposing that Orchises publish "Hapworth 16, 1924," as a book. Much to

Lathbury's surprise, Salinger responded that he would consider the proposal, signing his note J.D.S.

Nothing happened for eight years. In 1996, out of the blue, Lathbury received a letter from Salinger's literary agent, Harold Ober Associates, saying Salinger would soon be in touch. Sure enough, Lathbury soon received a "chatty, personal...sweet and endearing" note from Salinger, followed by a phone call. Salinger, the famous recluse, even proposed lunch at the National Gallery of Art in Washington.

Salinger, then 77, drove from Cornish to Washington, meeting Lathbury in a public cafeteria at the National Gallery. They stood in line to fetch their own food and ate quietly. Soon after, they signed an agreement to publish "Hapworth" in the first half of 1997.

It's not at all clear why Salinger wanted to publish a book version of "Hapworth," why he chose such an obscure publisher, or why he ventured out of his Cornish hideaway to meet Lathbury in such a public place.

In any case, fate intervened. A reporter for a local newspaper got wind of the deal, and the story was picked up by the *Washington Post* in January 1997. Lathbury had made the unforgivable mistake of talking to both newspapers, providing details about the book and about Salinger. The deal collapsed. Just after Salinger died in 2010, Lathbury told the full story of what happened in the March 31 issue of *New York Magazine*. It was called "Betraying Salinger."

Salinger never published another story after "Hapworth" appeared in 1965. Not in *The New Yorker* nor anyplace else. Though he lived for another forty-five years and wrote nearly every day, he kept all his work to himself.

Holden in the Rye

Considering its iconic status today, *The Catcher in the Rye* had a surprisingly arduous road to publication. Even when it was published in 1951, it gave no sign of becoming such an extraordinary, long-lasting success. The reviews were mixed, and though it sold well enough to make the *New York Times* bestseller list for twenty-nine weeks, it didn't rise above the number four slot, outpaced by *From Here to Eternity* by James Jones and *The Caine Mutiny* by Herman Wouk.[119]

Ten years in the making, *The Catcher in the Rye* was never far from Salinger's thoughts. He carried a copy of his work in progress throughout his time in the army, even packing chapters when he landed on Utah Beach in Normandy on D-Day, June 6, 1944.

Shortly before D-Day, Salinger had written to Whit Burnett, his mentor from Columbia, saying he had six stories featuring a character named Holden Caulfield, but he wanted to save them for a novel he was writing. He added that he wanted to narrate the novel in the first person, which would feel more personal and immediate. As it turned out, the first-person narrative amplified Salinger's gift for dialogue.[120]

Whit Burnett was encouraging, but he worried that Salinger was a short story writer, not a novelist. Salinger himself was concerned, calling himself "a dash man and not a miler."[121] In the end, he did construct *The Catcher in the Rye* as a series of short stories, nine in all, that he strung together.

The first time that the name Holden Caulfield appeared in print came soon after the war ended, when a story called "I'm Crazy" was published in *Collier's* in its December 1945 issue. Salinger folded most of the story into *The Catcher in the Rye*, released six years later. In all, at least eight of the short stories that Salinger wrote during the war years featured characters named Caulfield, including Holden and his brother Vincent. Some of the stories referred to a school called Pencey Prep, known to future readers as the school that flunked Holden Caulfield.

In 1949, Robert Giroux, then an editor at Harcourt, Brace & Company, wrote to Salinger in care of *The New Yorker*, suggesting that Harcourt publish a collection of his short stories. Salinger did not respond, and Giroux assumed he wasn't interested in the idea. Then, months later, Salinger showed up, unannounced, at Giroux's office. "A tall, sad-looking young man... walked in, saying 'It's not my short stories that should be published first, but the novel I'm working on.'"

"Do you want to sit behind this desk?" Giroux asked. "You sound just like a publisher."[122]

"No," Salinger replied, "you can do the stories later if you want, but I think my novel about this kid in New York during the Christmas holidays should come out first." Giroux agreed, and the two men shook hands. It was a deal, or so it seemed.

Giroux then brought the book to his superior, Eugene Reynal. Educated at Harvard and Oxford and listed in the *New York Social Register*, Reynal seemed too much the upper-crust socialite to appreciate the renegade Holden. Sure enough, Reynal balked with these words: "Is Holden Caulfield supposed to be crazy?" He thus passed up the opportunity to acquire a book that went on to become one of the most successful books ever published in the US. (In a show of ill-considered consistency, Harcourt Brace also rejected Jack Kerouac's *On the Road*, which was finally published in 1957, to great acclaim, by Viking Press.)

John Woodburn of Little, Brown could hardly believe his good luck when Harcourt declined *The Catcher in the Rye*. He snapped it up, as did Hamish Hamilton in England.

True to form, Salinger again proved difficult to deal with, even though his instincts were often right. For example, he insisted that the cover of the book should be designed by E. Michael Mitchell, a friend he had recently made while they both lived in Westport, Connecticut. The cover proved to be brilliant, famous for its depiction of a red carousel horse, like the one that Phoebe (Holden Caulfield's sister) rides in Central Park at the end of *The Catcher in the Rye*.

Mitchell and Salinger remained close friends long after *Catcher* was published. They corresponded for another forty years, and their letters are now housed at the Morgan Library in New York.[123]

Salinger also demanded that Little, Brown not send any advance proofs of the novel to book reviewers, a standard practice in the publishing industry. Because the proofs had already been dispatched, Salinger told Little, Brown not to forward him any reviews of the book. He declared he wouldn't do any publicity for the book—no interviews, no speeches, no appearances at all. Finally, Angus Cameron, chief editor at Little, Brown, said to Salinger, "Do you want this book published or just printed?"[124] Salinger relented, leaving for England when the book was published.

In a major surprise, the Book-of-the-Month Club (BOMC) made *The Catcher in the Rye* its main selection for its mid-summer distribution, a rare honor for a first book by a little-known author. Salinger was unimpressed but agreed to an interview with William Maxwell to be published in the BOMC News. In his piece, Maxwell gushed in decidedly non-*New Yorker* fashion about the book, comparing Salinger to Flaubert.[125] Similarly, Clifton Fadiman, a television pundit and BOMC judge, wrote: "That rare miracle of fiction has again come to pass: a human being has been created out of ink, paper, and the imagination."[126]

But that "rare miracle of fiction" received mixed reviews. There were negative notices in the *New Republic*, the *Christian Science Monitor*, and the *Nation*, and a mixed review in the *Atlantic Monthly*. The *New York Times* weighed in with two reviews— one in the Sunday *Book Review* that cleverly satirized the voice of Holden but was essentially negative,[127] the other in the daily *Times* that called *The Catcher in the Rye* "an unusually brilliant first novel."[128] *Time* magazine weighed in with an extremely positive review.

Salinger did not bask in any of the acclaim or bemoan any of the negative notices. He even demanded that Little, Brown remove his photograph from the back cover of the dust jacket. "Too big," he said.[129] Little, Brown complied in the third edition published soon after.

Footnote to history: Salinger's photo on the dust jacket of the first two editions of *The Catcher in the Rye* was taken in 1950 by Lotte Jacobi, best known for her photographic portraits of leading cultural figures. For some reason, her photo of Salinger was flipped, creating a mirror image of Salinger on the dust jacket of his most famous book. Nobody seems to know how it happened.

(The correct photo, with Salinger facing to his left, appears on the cover of this book, *Salinger's Soul*. It is in color, rather than the original black and white.)

• • •

Salinger's gift for dialogue is never more evident than in *The Catcher in the Rye*. He marvelously captures both the conversational voice of an anguished teenager and his inner musings, a stream of consciousness rich in meaning and fantasy.

Holden addresses the reader directly from a mental institution in California. He switches to flashbacks, starting with his final days at Pencey Prep in Pennsylvania. After flunking out, he heads to New York City for a two-day odyssey in which he encounters a couple of nuns, several cab drivers, many tourists, a former classmate, numerous women in bars, and various other characters in mid-century New York.

In the words of critic Paul Levine, Holden is the "Misfit Hero."[130] At sixteen, he is neither child nor adult. "Sometimes I act like I'm about 13," he admits. He resists growing up, so as not to lose his idealized notion of childhood and the innocence and authenticity that come with it. In its place, he fears an adult world of depredation, requiring compromise with all the jerks and phonies lurking about. Far from being a coming-of-age story, *The Catcher in the Rye* is the story of a refusal to come of age.

Wandering around New York, he sees the Christmas show at Radio City Music Hall, watches a movie there, and skates on the nearby ice-skating rink, some of the time with a girl he knows, Sally Hayes. He asks himself where the ducks in Central Park go when their pond freezes in the winter. "I wondered if some guy came in a truck and took them away to a zoo or something."

He's full of bravado about sex, but his anxiety shows when he hires a prostitute in his hotel, then refuses to have sex with her. His compassion shows, too. "I thought of her going in a store and buying [the dress] and nobody in the store knowing she was a prostitute... It made me feel sad as hell—I don't know why exactly."

Her pimp, the hotel elevator man, then beats him up. "I really felt like...committing suicide. I felt like jumping out the window. I probably would have done it, too, if I'd been sure somebody'd cover me up as soon as I landed. I didn't want a bunch of stupid rubbernecks looking at me when I was all gory."

He soon visits the Museum of Natural History, the very repository of a world that doesn't change, doesn't grow up:

> "You could go there a hundred thousand times, and that Eskimo would still be just finished catching those two fish, the birds would still be on their way south, the deers would still be drinking out of that water hole, with their pretty antlers and their pretty, skinny legs, and that squaw with the naked bosom would still

be weaving that same blanket. Nobody'd
be different..."

And that is just fine with Holden:

"Certain things they should stay the way
they are. You ought to be able to stick
them in one of those big glass cases and
just leave them alone."

Along the way, he sees a little boy, about six, singing
a song: "If a body catch a body coming through the
rye." "It made me feel better," Holden thinks. "It made
me feel not so depressed anymore."

Holden mourns his brother Allie, who died of leu-
kemia when he was eleven and Holden was thirteen. "I
slept in the garage the night he died, and broke all the
goddam windows with my fist, just for the hell of it..."
He cherishes Allie's baseball glove, which is adorned
with poems Allie had written in green ink, so he'd have
something to read while playing the outfield in the
game's slower moments.

He dismisses his older brother D. B., a successful
Hollywood screenwriter, as a "prostitute." Says Holden:
"He just got a Jaguar. One of those little English jobs
that can do around 200 miles an hour." Still, D. B. visits
him nearly every week at "this crumby place," the mental institution that is home to Holden for the time being.

Above all, he loves his younger sister, Phoebe, who is
ten. Visiting her school, he sees "Fuck you" written on

a wall. "It drove me damn near crazy," Holden muses. "I thought how Phoebe and the other little kids would see it, and how they'd wonder what the hell it meant, and then finally some dirty kid would tell them—all cockeyed, naturally—what it meant...I kept wanting to kill whoever'd written it..."

Holden explains to Phoebe his fantasy of being a catcher in the rye:

> "I'm standing on the edge of some crazy cliff. What I have to do, I have to catch everybody if they start to go over the cliff—I mean if they're running and they don't look where they're going, I have to come out from somewhere and catch them. That's all I'd do all day. I'd just be the catcher in the rye and all. I know it's crazy but that's the only thing I'd like to be."

But Phoebe, remarkable for her age, tells her beloved brother that he is misinterpreting the poem by Robert Burns, which doesn't mean what Holden thinks it means. "When a body *meets* a body coming through the rye," she informs him—not *catch* a body. Near the end, Holden takes Phoebe to the carousel in Central Park, sitting in the rain watching her go round and round.

"I felt so damn happy all of a sudden...I don't know why. It was just that she looked so damn *nice*...in her blue coat and all. I wish you could have been there."

As Holden watches Phoebe riding the carousel in Central Park, said critic Harold Bloom, it "evokes Nick Carraway at Gatsby's funeral, and Frederic Henry walking away after Catherine's death, in *A Farewell to Arms*."[131] "This Phoebe is one of the most exquisitely created and engaging child in any novel," added S. N. Behrman in his review of *Catcher* in *The New Yorker*.[132]

Holden is done telling his story. He's still in the mental institution, unsure of what comes next after he goes home:

> "About all I know is, I sort of *miss* everybody... Don't ever tell anybody anything. If you do, you'll start missing everybody."

●●●

It took a while for *The Catcher in the Rye* to become a legendary success, but by the late 1950s and 1960s, many high school and college students began identifying with Holden's alienation from society. They saw him as a rebel with a cause, a troubled teenager who became an anguished protestor against the sterility, materialism, and conformity of the 1950s. *Catcher* "had become the book all brooding adolescents had to buy, the indispensable manual from which cool styles of disaffection could be borrowed," wrote Ian Hamilton in his Salinger biography.[133]

And, like me, perhaps we all just sympathized with Holden's manifest difficulty in growing up. After all, it was safe to like Holden because he wasn't really a radical out to overthrow the system. The book's argument, wrote Warren G. French, a literary critic, "is that the world is generally phony," "but that it must be accepted as it is by individuals who must work out their own salvation."[134]

In a cover story on Salinger in 1961, a decade later, *Time* magazine put it similarly: "Holden is not a rebel. He longs to do good in the world. When he broods about dirty words on a wall where little children can see them, or feels compassion for a prostitute, he is not protesting against the system...he is merely suffering from the way things are...in a world of insufficient love."[135]

Even fifty years after publication, critics were having their say. Louis Menand, who was then teaching at Harvard, wrote that Salinger's withdrawal from public life two years after *Catcher* was issued "helped to confirm the belief that Holden's unhappiness was less personal...that it was really some sort of protest against modern life."[136]

One unusual interpretation is that *The Catcher in the Rye* is really a war novel. "Holden Caulfield has more in common with a traumatized soldier than [with] an alienated teenager," said Andy Rogers, who wrote about *Catcher* in his PhD thesis at the University of Alabama. It was published in 2008 as a paperback book called *The Veteran Who Is, the Boy Who Is No More*. Rogers argued that Salinger, damaged by his own war experience, disguised his depression in a more universal context, the anguish of a sixteen-year-old boy at war with society and with himself.

Another way I've tried to understand Salinger's masterpiece is to ask a basic question: What if *The Catcher in the Rye* had been published now? Would readers embrace it with similar fervor? Or would it seem hopelessly outdated, a time capsule from mid-century America that seems irrelevant today? In short, does Holden Caulfield speak to today's readers the way he once did?

Yes, "if you're a white, relatively affluent, permanently grouchy young man," wrote *Electric Literature*, a digital quarterly that publishes essays, criticism, and fiction on digital platforms. "But for the majority of readers who are not young, not white, and not male," you probably "can't stand listening to Holden Caulfield feel sorry for himself."[137] In other words, in the diverse, complicated world of twenty-first-century America, it's possible that a newly introduced Holden Caulfield would just be an out-of-place anomaly.

Literary critic Alfred Kazin made a similar point when he wrote that Holden is simply immature, that Salinger is confusing the familiar rebellion of an adolescent with something more profound.[138]

Many ordinary readers of *Catcher* also criticized the book, voicing their displeasure in later years on Amazon's website. Roland E. Miller, an English teacher, posted a familiar joke in July 2014: "If I had written this book, I would have gone into hiding too."

Moreover, times have changed, said novelist Dana Czapnik. "How can one get all worked up about some 'phony' classmate...when earlier that morning you did an active-shooter drill in your classroom."[139]

Perhaps. But you could say much the same thing about *The Great Gatsby*: why would anyone care these days about a flapper-age social climber who invents a new name and persona in a futile attempt to win the rich woman of his dreams? Why, for that matter, care even about *Hamlet*, the saga of an indecisive Danish prince who seeks to avenge the murder of his royal father, written more than four hundred years ago?

Well, we do care: even period pieces qualify as works of art if they're good enough. And to judge by *The Catcher in the Rye*'s blockbuster sales to this day, a lot of people agree. What other book, having sold over sixty-five million copies since it was published more than seventy years ago, still manages to sell some two hundred thousand copies a year?[140] Every year.

CHAPTER 9

From Seymour to Teddy

In April 1953, two years after *The Catcher in the Rye* was published, Little, Brown released Salinger's second book, *Nine Stories*. Each of the stories had already been published, seven of them in *The New Yorker*. But bound together, they brought fresh attention to Salinger. And read together, they seemed to share common attributes and reinforce themes that fascinated Salinger.[141]

All the stories feature dialogue, the colloquial voice that distinguishes nearly all of Salinger's fiction. The dialogue is often between an adult and a child— for example, between Seymour Glass and Sybil in "A Perfect Day for Bananafish"; between Sergeant X and Esmé in "For Esmé—with Love and Squalor"; between Boo Boo Tannenbaum and her son, Lionel, in "Down at the Dinghy"; and between Nicholson and Teddy in "Teddy." The adults are often jaded, the children full of innocence. Several of the stories deal with alienation and disaffection, as well as the fear of lost innocence amid the woes of the adult world, a prominent earlier theme in *The Catcher in the Rye*.

Salinger also tried to infuse these stories with spirituality and religion. The epigraph he quoted at the start of *Nine Stories* is the famous Zen riddle known as a koan:

"We know the sound of two hands clapping.

But what is the sound of one hand clapping?"

According to some scholars, Salinger intended all nine stories to be read as riddles—as Zen koans that are points of departure for thinking, questioning, and meditating. A koan can have two outcomes: the struggle to understand can lead to a sudden form of enlightenment known as *satori* (as in "For Esmé—with Love and Squalor" or "De Daumier-Smith's Blue Period"). Or it can lead to a mental breakdown (as in "A Perfect Day for Bananafish" or "Teddy"). In this view, the nine stories are really koan experiences that require asking more and more questions.[142]

• • •

"Teddy," published in *The New Yorker* just before *Nine Stories* was released, is especially shocking. The story is about Teddy, a ten-year-old boy genius, and his sister, Booper, who is six. They are on a cruise with their parents when Teddy meets a passenger named Bob Nicholson. In a philosophical conversation, the precocious boy talks about his lack of emotion:

"I take it you have no emotions?" Nicholson asks.

"If I do, I don't remember when I ever used them," Teddy replies. "I don't see what they're good for."

Teddy goes on to tell Nicholson that he can see in his mind how and when a certain person will die:

"All you do is get the heck out of your body when you die," Teddy tells Nicholson. "My gosh, everybody's done it thousands and thousands of times..."

"For example, I have a swimming lesson in about five minutes. I could go downstairs to the pool, and there might not be any water in it...I might walk up to the edge of it, just to have a look at the bottom, for instance, and my sister might come up and sort of push me in. I could fracture my skull and die instantly."

When Teddy leaves for his swimming lesson, Nicholson soon follows him.

"He was little more than halfway down the staircase when he heard an all-piercing sustained scream—clearly coming from a small, female child. It was highly acoustical, as though it were reverberating within four tiled walls."

The story ends and the reader is left wondering: Did his sister push him into the empty pool, as Teddy imagined in his conversation with Nicholson? Or did Teddy push his sister in, thus demonstrating his lack of emotion? Or was it an accident; either one of them could have fallen in. Or jumped.

I was as confused as anyone. But many critics claim it's clear that Teddy killed himself. In this view, Teddy is an early incarnation of Seymour, a seer with mystical views who commits suicide. Thus, *Nine Stories* starts and ends with a suicide. "By making us understand Teddy's attitude, Salinger makes us understand that it is Teddy who [jumps]," wrote literary critic Arthur Mizener in *Harper's* magazine in 1959,[143] when I was a college student still trying to figure it out.

No surprise, Salinger received more mail about "Teddy" than for any short story he ever wrote, with the possible exception of "For Esmé—with Love and Squalor." Many readers initially took the story at face value, focusing on the enigmatic ending.

But Salinger had religion in mind. Teddy is enlightened, focused on inner spirituality and Godliness, while his parents are materialistic and concerned with outward appearances. And by embracing the Vedantic philosophy of reincarnation, Teddy may die but he will return as a new person—making suicide acceptable.

Teddy believes the body is just a shell and that external things are not real. Only unity with God is real.

"Teddy" was Salinger's most important step in bringing religious mysticism to his stories. Yet very few critics reviewing the story mentioned anything remotely Zen. Overall, they were decidedly mixed, which didn't stop *Nine Stories* from reaching the *New York Times'* bestseller list. Charles Poore, in the daily *New York Times*, hated the book, though he did rave about "Esmé," calling it "the best short story to have come out of World War II."[144] At the other extreme, Eudora Welty, a renowned short-story writer, loved *Nine Stories*, writing in the *New York Times Book Review* that Salinger was a "born writer" with "a sensitive eye" and "a great ear."[145]

One of the most perceptive reviews came from Gilbert Highet in *Harper's*. He saw in each of the nine stories a "thin, nervous, intelligent being who is on the verge of breakdown: we see him at various stages of his life, as a child, as an adolescent, as an aimless young man in his twenties."[146] Like Salinger himself, the characters—from Lionel and Teddy to Seymour and Sergeant X—add up to a serialized self-portrait of a man in distress, sometimes to the point of suicide.

The reviews in Britain were favorable, in contrast to the generally frosty reception that greeted *The Catcher in the Rye* two years earlier. Hamish Hamilton, the British publisher, retitled the book "For Esmé—with Love and Squalor," thinking it would sell better.

Salinger reluctantly agreed to the name change from *Nine Stories*, and all went well with the hardcover version. However, when the paperback was published soon after, Salinger had a falling out with Jamie Hamish Hamilton, the founder and proprietor of his namesake publishing company.[147]

Jamie Hamilton had been Salinger's trusted professional friend, a close second to William Shawn of *The New Yorker*. Hamilton had handled the British publication of *The Catcher in the Rye* to the satisfaction of the hard-to-please Salinger. But this time, there was trouble. Hamilton tried to contract the paperback rights of *For Esmé—with Love and Squalor* to Penguin Books, which had published the British paperback of *Catcher*. But it declined *Esmé*. He then sold the rights to Harborough Publishing, whose paperback imprint, Ace Books, proceeded to publish the retitled *Esmé— with Love and Squalor* with special emphasis on *squalor*. The garish cover depicted a sleazy blond woman, much older than the thirteen-year-old Esmé. Above her head it said: "EXPLOSIVE AND ABSORBING. A PAINFUL AND PITIABLE GALLERY OF MEN, WOMEN, ADOLESCENTS AND CHILDREN."

When Salinger saw the tawdry British paperback months later, he felt betrayed. Hamilton conceded the cover was of "singular vulgarity," but claimed he, the hardcover publisher, had no control over the paperback cover design.[148] His efforts to assuage Salinger failed, and the two men, once good friends, never spoke again.

The feud obscured the fact that most English critics liked the retitled *Nine Stories*, often discussing Salinger's focus on the relationship between children and adults. Salinger, wrote the *Observer*, "seems to understand children as no English-speaking writer has done since Lewis Carroll.[149]

Salinger's growing obsession with children had a purpose. From a Zen perspective, children are, almost by definition, enlightened. They tend to be spontaneous and imaginative, free of the responsibilities, ego, and logical thinking that often limit the freedom and independence of adults. Put another way, children live in a non-sequitur world, unburdened by the constraints of logic.

To Salinger, *Nine Stories* was just the start of his quest for spiritual understanding. It pervaded nearly all the fiction he published from then on.

CHAPTER 10

Retreat to Cornish

In early 1953, following the great success of *The Catcher in the Rye*, and with *Nine Stories* about to be published, Salinger longed for privacy. He wanted the isolation his writing required, as well as the time and space for meditation. All the attention he got after *The Catcher in the Rye*, he said, was "professionally and personally de-moralizing." He longed for the day, he joked, when he'd see the dust jacket of *Catcher* "flapping against a lamp post in a cold, wet Lexington Avenue wind, in company with, say, the editorial page of the *Daily Mirror*."[150]

He asked Doris, his older sister, to accompany him on a drive to New England to look for a suitable place—not a weekend getaway, but a permanent house to call home. They stopped for lunch in Windsor, Vermont, where a local real estate broker drove them across a covered bridge to the hamlet of Cornish, New Hampshire, about 250 miles from New York City. The bridge was said to be the longest covered bridge in the United States, but Cornish itself barely existed: no bank, no post office, no stores, no village life. Once upon a time, in the late nineteenth century, Cornish had had its moment as an artists' colony centered on Augustus Saint-Gaudens, a respected sculptor best known for his statues in the Boston Commons and Central Park in New York. Other than that, Cornish's main claim to fame was that it had served as the summer White House for President Woodrow Wilson from 1913 to 1915.[151]

There, in the middle of nowhere, Salinger and Doris saw a ramshackle red barn sitting on a ninety-acre site in Cornish, much of it in the woods. The barn had a makeshift living area and a small kitchen, but no heat, no running water. There was, however, a stunning view of the Connecticut River Valley. Salinger decided to buy it. Doris later told her niece, Salinger's daughter, "It wasn't a house, Peggy. It was a disaster."[152]

But it satisfied Salinger's need for privacy. As he later wrote on the dust jacket of *Franny and Zooey*:

> "It is my rather subversive opinion that
> a writer's feelings of anonymity/obscurity
> are the second most valuable property on
> loan to him during his working years."

Salinger soon got to work on the house. He cut wood for the fireplace and hauled water from a nearby stream. Because he had no phone, Salinger relied on his closest neighbors, a local artist named Bertrand Yeaton and his wife, for any important messages. But he managed to have the barn renovated into something livable, and he built a bunker in the woods, about a hundred yards from the house, as a writing studio. As Yeaton described it to *Newsweek*'s Mel Elfin, the bunker was made of concrete cinder blocks painted green to blend into the surrounding woods.[153] It had a wood-burning stove, a skylight, and a long table Salinger used as a desk. On the walls, he hung cup hooks, to which he clipped pages of notes for his stories. "He also has a ledger," Yeaton told Elfin, "to which he has pasted sheets of type-written manuscript on one page and... the opposite one has arrows, memos, and other notes for revision."

The hermit had found his hermitage.

In some ways, the Cornish house was a case of life imitating art. Two years earlier, in *The Catcher in the Rye*, Holden fantasized about building "a little cabin somewhere with the dough I made and live there for the rest of my life. I'd build it right near the woods, but not right *in* them, because I'd want it to be sunny as hell all the time."

At first, Salinger wasn't a recluse. He drove his Jeep nearly every day across the covered bridge to Windsor, Vermont, picking up his mail, buying supplies, talking to the townspeople, visiting their homes, and hosting them at his house. Windsor held a special irony for Salinger: It was once home to Maxwell Perkins, the legendary book editor at Scribner who had published the novels of F. Scott Fitzgerald, Salinger's literary hero, as well as the novels of Ernest Hemingway, Salinger's war-time friend.

At times Salinger stopped for coffee at Nap's Lunch or at the Harrington Spa, where he befriended a group of high school students, often inviting them to his house, where they played records and talked of school, sports, and their social lives. He went to their sporting events and hosted a youth group at the local church.

In November 1953, one of the high school students, a senior named Shirlie Blaney, asked Salinger if she could interview him for a school project. He agreed, and the two met for lunch at the Harrington Spa. Her questions were straightforward enough, but when she asked if *The Catcher in the Rye* was autobiographical, Salinger replied, "Sort of...My boyhood was very much the same as that of the boy in the book, and it was a great relief telling people about it.[154] This was not the sort of thing Salinger usually talked about.

Soon after, much to Salinger's surprise, the interview appeared not as a school project, but as a scoop in the local newspaper, the *Daily Eagle*. I don't know whether Blaney had deceived Salinger, or whether the newspaper decided to play up an exclusive interview with the famous author in their midst, or whether Salinger underestimated what his celebrity meant in small-town America. In any case, the story got picked up around the country. Salinger felt hurt, his privacy invaded, his trust undermined. He ended his relationship with the students, avoided the townspeople, and retreated into his shell. Soon after, he built a six-foot-high fence around his property.

Once again, Salinger showed how unforgiving he could be when he felt offended, repeating the behavior he demonstrated earlier against Whit Burnett, his Columbia mentor, A. E. Hotchner, his post-war friend in New York, and Jamie Hamilton, his London publisher. All were good friends—until they weren't.

Salinger did make new friends in Cornish, including Judge Learned Hand, a renowned Federal appellate court judge and legal scholar—perhaps the most famous judge who never made it to the Supreme Court. Judge Hand, in his eighties when Salinger met him, spent summers near Cornish. The two became good friends, and Judge Hand was godfather to Peggy, born in 1955. By marvelous coincidence, Judge Hand also had an abiding interest in Zen Buddhism and other Eastern religions.

They corresponded over the winter months, and Salinger confided in one letter to Judge Hand that he feared his preoccupation with Eastern religions might interfere with his writing: He wondered, he wrote, "whether I'm still [plying] my trade as a short story writer or whether I've gone over to propagandizing for the loin-cloth group."[155] He sometimes wished he could return to his old way of writing, he said. But he knew he couldn't, that he was consumed by his new God-seeking passion, especially in the Glass family stories.[156]

Judge Hand died at age eighty-nine on August 18, 1961, a month before *Franny and Zooey* was published.

•••

After Salinger moved to Cornish, he resumed his friendship with a teenager named Claire Douglas. He had met her a couple of years earlier in New York, at a party given by his friend, Francis Steegmuller, a writer at *The New Yorker*, and his wife, Beatrice Stein, an artist. It so happened that Claire's parents lived in the same apartment building as the Steegmullers—friends as well as neighbors—and Claire attended the party.[157] She was in high school at the time, a student at the Shipley School in Bryn Mawr, Pennsylvania. Though Salinger was in his thirties, he seemed interested in Claire and wrote to her at Shipley. They became friends, seeing each other occasionally while Claire finished boarding school.

Salinger soon learned her backstory: Born in London on November 17, 1933, Claire was raised by a governess. When the Germans started bombing England in 1940, Claire, six, and her half-brother, Gavin, eight, were sent to the country for safety, while their parents remained in London. For a time, Claire lived in a convent. A few months later, the family's London home was destroyed by Nazi planes, and Claire and Gavin were soon shipped to the United States on the *Scythia*, regularly used to ferry British children to safety.

During their wartime stay in America, Claire and Gavin lived in eight different foster homes. Their parents also lived in the US at the time but stayed in an apartment in New York without their children. Why the separation? I wondered. No one seems to know, and Claire never provided an explanation when Peggy asked her mother about it years later.[158] The wartime separation, combined with years of boarding school in the US, meant that Claire rarely lived with her family. Her father, Robert Langton Douglas, was a well-known art critic, mostly in London. Thirty-five years older than her mother, Jean Douglas, he died when Claire was in boarding school in Pennsylvania.

Flash forward to 1953. Claire was now a student at Radcliffe and Salinger was ensconced in his new home in Cornish. They saw each other regularly, sometimes during weekends in Cornish, according to Peggy.[159]

Problem was, Salinger was not the only man in Claire's life. The other guy was Colman Mockler, Jr., a twenty-three-year-old MBA student at the Harvard Business School—an attractive, bright, and sensitive rival.[160] When Salinger became aware of Mockler, he tried to convince Claire to drop out of Radcliffe and live with him in Cornish. She refused, travelling with Mockler to Europe in the summer of 1953. When she returned in September, Salinger, angry at Claire, was nowhere to be found. Claire assumed he had left the country.

When Claire was hospitalized with glandular fever in early 1954, it was Mockler who was at her bedside, helping to nurse her back to health. Salinger was never in touch. Mockler proposed marriage, Claire said yes, and the two were quickly married. It was soon clear that the marriage was a mistake, not least because Mockler had become a fundamentalist Christian, an uneasy fit with Claire's Salinger-inspired interest in Zen Buddhism and Vedantic Hinduism. A few months later, Claire resumed dating Salinger, and her marriage to Mockler was annulled.

For the record, Mockler went on to a distinguished career, becoming CEO of the Gillette Company and a major philanthropist, while maintaining a rich family life and deep religious belief.

Salinger renewed his effort to get Claire to leave college and move in with him in Cornish. This time, he succeeded. Claire dropped out of Radcliffe, just four months short of graduation. They were married in Vermont on February 17, 1955, and the marriage certificate claimed she was Salinger's first wife, thereby excommunicating his German war bride, Sylvia Welter. Claire, too, rewrote history, naming Salinger as her first husband.[161]

As a wedding gift, Salinger gave Claire a special copy of "Franny," his newest story in *The New Yorker*. It was clear that the character of Franny was modeled in many ways on Claire: for one thing, it was Claire's favorite book, *The Way of a Pilgrim*, that Franny clutches in

The New Yorker story. The next day, Salinger, acting completely out of character, held a house party to celebrate the wedding. Among the guests: his mother, Miriam; sister, Doris; and, of all people, Colman Mockler.[162] Salinger's father, Sol, was conspicuous by his absence, further evidence of his continuing estrangement from his son.

For Claire, the isolated rural existence in Cornish was hard to endure. In June 1955, S. J. Perelman, Salinger's colleague at *The New Yorker*, visited the couple in Cornish, later describing their habitat as a "private mountaintop overlooking five states."

Then in a letter to their mutual friend, Leila Hadley, Perelman wrote:

> "It's anybody's guess how long his
> wife—young, passably pretty—will want
> to endure the solitude...Jerry, in all jus-
> tice, looked better than I've ever seen
> him, so evidently he's flourishing [in]
> matrimony."[163]

Married life seemed normal at first. Claire and Jerry went to town meetings, enjoyed film screenings at Dartmouth College, just twenty miles away, and visited neighbors, including Judge Learned Hand. They continued to see friends, and Claire occasionally accompanied him on his frequent trips to New York. Encouraged by Jerry, Claire furthered her interest in Buddhism and

Vedanta, becoming a modest practitioner. She meditated, performed yoga, and read, sometimes with Jerry, such books as *The Gospel of Sri Ramakrishna* and *The Autobiography of a Yogi*.[164]

Most days, Salinger worked on his next story, "Raise High the Roofbeam, Carpenters." Up by 6:00 AM, he ate breakfast, packed his lunch, then went to his writing bunker, where he worked nonstop—draft after draft—until dinnertime, often returning to his bunker after dinner. He had a phone installed in his bunker, along with an army cot, but made it clear to Claire he didn't want to be disturbed for anything less than a dire emergency.[165] Sometimes, he stayed in the bunker overnight, even for days on end. Later in his marriage, even the bunker didn't provide sufficient distance. In 1958 and 1959, he frequently took off for New York, writing in hotel rooms or at *The New Yorker*, working late into the night.

On December 22, 1955, less than a year after their wedding, Claire gave birth to their first child, Margaret, soon known as Peggy. Claire was twenty-two, Jerry nearly thirty-seven. By all accounts, Salinger doted on Peggy. When she grew older, Salinger often took her with him when he visited New York. They usually stayed at the Plaza Hotel, spending a lot of time visiting "Holden's New York"—seeing the dinosaurs at the American Museum of Natural History, visiting the duck pond in Central Park, and riding the carousel. He even took her to lunch with *New Yorker* editor William Shawn and his paramour, Lillian Ross.[166]

At the same time, he paid less and less attention to Claire, according to accounts by Peggy in her memoir written years later. As Claire herself said, she and Salinger rarely had sex. She was no longer the virginal teenager that had first attracted his interest, no longer the prototype of the young women Salinger found attractive. As Salinger once wrote about a fictional character, she was no longer in "the last minute of her girlhood."[167]

Worse, Peggy said, Salinger was abusive to her mother. He refused to allow Claire to see friends and family and demanded special meals of organic food. Mostly, Peggy wrote, her mother was quite lonely because Salinger spent most of his time in his writing bunker. Doris told Peggy that when Claire became pregnant, she had "a suicidal depression when she realized that her pregnancy only repulsed him." In 1957, during a trip to New York, Claire took the infant Peggy and left Salinger. Supported by her stepfather, she lived apart for four months—before giving in to Salinger's plea to return to Cornish. Things only got worse after Matthew was born in 1960.

In short, S. J. Perelman was right. Claire could not endure the deprivations that came with marriage to Salinger: the long days he spent in his writing bunker; the nights he sometimes slept there; his frequent trips without her; his peculiar habits and demands; the isolation of Cornish; his writing-above-all-else attitude. By 1966, Claire, no longer able to cope, sought the help of a local doctor, and soon after filed for divorce in Newport, New Hampshire. A year later, in October 1967, the divorce was granted, officially ending twelve years of marriage.

Claire was given custody of the children, child support payments, use of the house and property, and the promise that Salinger would pay the tuition for private school and college for Peggy and Matt.[168] Salinger retained a nearby property, which became his new home, just walking distance from the house he had bought in 1953. He gave up his writing bunker, building a new studio above his new garage. He saw the children frequently and maintained a civil relationship with Claire.

After her divorce, Claire enrolled at Goddard College in nearby Plainfield, Vermont, to finish the undergraduate degree she had abandoned at Radcliffe when she left to live with Salinger. After receiving her bachelor's degree in 1969, she earned two master's degrees: one in education at another local college, the other in social work at the Rochester Institute of Technology (while her children were away in prep school). Finally, Claire received a PhD from the Saybrook Institute in San Francisco in 1984, enabling her to be a child psychologist, starting at age fifty-one.[169]

In 1991, Claire Douglas moved her practice to New York, renting an apartment on the Upper East Side.

One neighbor, George Plimpton, remembered her as "very, very pretty...blond, very gracious, very soft-spoken." He said that "in all of the time she lived in that apartment, three or four years, we never once, not once, discussed Salinger."[170]

Peggy was then living in Boston and Matt was an actor, often in theater roles in New York. Later, when Matt's acting career shifted mainly to Hollywood, Claire moved to Los Angeles to be nearer to Matt and his family. She became an affiliate of the C. G. Jung Institute of Los Angeles, in Malibu, writing many scholarly books, most of them on women and children. In an ironic twist, I learned, she published more books than Salinger ever did. She never remarried—and she has never spoken publicly about her life with Salinger.

●●●

After Claire and the children moved away, Salinger continued writing every day. Perhaps there's no connection, but he never published anything after Claire left the marriage. His sister, Doris, said he stopped publishing because he couldn't stand the inevitable criticism.

Maybe so, but I think there's more to it. Always hostile to the publishing process, he disliked most editors and publishers, declined to do anything to promote his books, and couldn't stand the attendant publicity that came with the release of a new book. In 1970, he withdrew from his contract with Little, Brown, returning a hefty $75,000 advance he had gotten for his next book, the equivalent of some $600,000 nowadays.[171]

Salinger did move on to a new life. He wrote nearly every day, but without publishing any of it, he could easily stay out of the public eye. So much so that hardly anyone knew Salinger had remarried until October 1992, when a fire nearly destroyed Salinger's house in Cornish. Fire trucks arrived on the scene after a caller to the Fire Department identified herself as Mrs. Salinger. It was Colleen O'Neill Salinger, who had been married to Salinger since 1988. They were together in Cornish for the last twenty-two years of his life.[172]

CHAPTER 11

Religious Zeal

It was in Cornish that Salinger's fiction focused entirely on the Glass family, especially four of the seven siblings: Franny, Zooey, Buddy, and Seymour. All the stories were infused with religion in one way or another: mystical Christianity at first, then Hinduism and Zen Buddhism, and finally Vedanta, an offshoot of Hinduism.

There is nothing about Judaism, what Claire called the other "ism," in the Glass saga after *Nine Stories*, even though the siblings had a Jewish father, Les Glass, and a gentile mother, Bess Gallagher, just as Jerry Salinger did.[173] In fact, the Glass family was even less Jewish than the Salinger's. None of the four sons had a bar mitzvah, and one of them converted to Catholicism. The other children were tutored in Vedanta Hinduism by Seymour.

Overall, Salinger wrote only two stories that contained anything at all Jewish:

In "A Girl I Knew," published in *Good Housekeeping* magazine in 1948, Salinger fictionalizes the true story of a young woman he knew in Vienna just before the Nazi takeover in 1938. The woman, known as Leah in the story, lived with her family in the Jewish quarter of Vienna. All were killed by the Nazis. (See chapter 1.)

The second example of something Jewish in Salinger's fiction also deals with anti-Semitism, this time in America. In "Down at the Dinghy," a short story published in *Harper's* in April 1949 and reprinted in *Nine Stories*, Lionel, a four-year-old boy, threatens to run away from home. The family's housekeeper, Mrs. Snell, is talking about Lionel to a maid, Sondra:

> "He's kind of a good-looking kid," said Mrs. Snell. "Them big brown eyes and all." Sandra snorted again. "He's gonna have a big nose, just like his father."

At that point, Lionel's mother Boo Boo Tannenbaum (a sister of the other Glass siblings) tries to find out why Lionel wants to run away. He won't say, but starts to sob:

> "Sandra told Mrs. Snell that Daddy's a big sloppy kike."
> "Do you know what a kike is, baby?"

"It's one of those things that go up in
the air, he said. With a string you hold."

To a four-year-old boy, a *kike* is a *kite*—a sad-comic
way for Salinger to present a problem beyond a boy's
ken. There's no further mention of anti-Semitism or of
Jews in the story. But to Salinger's daughter, Peggy, the
story is evidence of her father's "touchiness" about his
own Jewishness, buttressing Doris's view that he had
experienced at least some anti-Semitism growing up in
the 1920s and 1930s.

Still, these are scant references to anything Jewish in
a lifetime of writing.

Referring to "Down at the Dinghy," literary critic
Ihab Hassan wrote in 1957: "Is this all that so gifted
an author can do with the deep-down complexity of a
Jew's fate in our culture?"[174]

●●●

After "Down at the Dinghy," Salinger devoted himself
to various religious themes. In "Franny," published in
The New Yorker in its January 29, 1955, issue, we meet
Franny (no last name), a student at an unnamed wom-
en's college (like Wellesley) who is away for a football
weekend at some Ivy League school (like Princeton).
Her date for the weekend is Lane Coutrell, a student
much obsessed with himself and full of intellectual pre-
tensions. While he eats frog's legs at lunch with Franny
before the Yale game, she explains that she's experienc-

ing some sort of religious ecstasy over a book called *The Way of a Pilgrim*.

She describes the book to Lane this way: An anonymous Russian peasant roams the land teaching the Jesus Prayer: "Lord Jesus Christ have mercy on me." Says Franny: "If you keep saying that prayer over and over again...something *happens* after a while...the words get synchronized with the person's heartbeats..."

Something certainly happens to Franny. After fleeing to a restroom with nausea and anxiety, she faints, she is revived, and she faints again, ending up lying on the bar staring at the ceiling and soundlessly mouthing the Jesus prayer again and again. In typical Salinger fashion, the story ends then and there. When it first appeared in *The New Yorker*, readers were left to guess what had happened to her and what came next. Many speculated she was pregnant. She wasn't, as even Salinger later acknowledged.[175]

"Franny" was taut, stylishly written, and just plain engaging. And Franny herself voices some of Salinger's pet peeves, about self-importance and ambition:

> "I'm just sick of ego, ego, ego. My own and everybody else's. I'm sick of everybody who wants to *get* somewhere, do something distinguished and all, be somebody interesting. It's disgusting—it is, it *is*. I don't care what anybody says."

"Franny" became even more popular on college campuses than *The Catcher in the Rye*, partly because Salinger, the college dropout, attacked academic pretense. Critic Warren French called "Franny" a "devastating satire" about "a world that is full of pedants eager to display their erudition rather than...pilgrims still seeking to learn."[176]

"Zooey" appeared as a kind of sequel to "Franny" in *The New Yorker* two years later. This time around, Franny has taken to the couch in the Glass family living room, clutching her copy of *The Way of a Pilgrim* and petting her cat, Bloomberg (which draws a laugh now that it didn't then). Zooey, her handsome actor brother, is brilliant, funny, and eloquent to the point of disbelief. "A verbal stunt pilot," says one Glass sibling. In one remarkable scene that takes seventy-one pages, their Irish mother, Bessie, engages Zooey in a bathroom conversation, she sitting on the closed toilet seat while he is taking a bath behind the shower curtain.

When Zooey tries to rally Franny, he initially invokes her fascination with the Jesus Prayer, but it fails to help. He then tries to talk her out of her spiritual crisis via long monologues invoking spirituality, Christianity, and Buddhism. Toward the end of the story, he succeeds by appealing to her religious instincts in a way that recalls her revered brother, Seymour, the family guru and ghost, who killed himself years earlier in Salinger's short story, "A Perfect Day for Bananafish." It was Seymour, of course, who preached Eastern mysticism so that his worshipful siblings later gave the impression, wrote John Skow in *Time* magazine, "that they had played catch with some West Side version of Buddha."[177]

As Zooey tells her, when the Glass siblings were child prodigies on a radio quiz show, Seymour insisted that they shine their shoes even though nobody listening on the radio could see their shoes. Why? "For the Fat Lady," he says, all those ordinary people out there who are lonely, unattractive, and invisible. "There isn't anyone out there who isn't Seymour's Fat Lady...Don't you know that goddam secret yet?...Don't you know who that Fat Lady really is?...Ah, buddy, it's Christ himself. Christ himself, buddy."

This is supposed to be some sort of religious revelation, which somehow convinces Franny to rouse herself out of her stupor. Perhaps Salinger's message was simple: that we should all love the unattractive Fat Ladies of the world, for they too are God's creatures. But just about everyone else who didn't share Franny's religious ecstasy, including many critics and countless readers like me, threw up their hands in confusion.

The two stories were linked together in the 1961 book, *Franny and Zooey*, and Salinger had high hopes for it. On the jacket flap of the book, he wrote:

> "Both stories are early, critical entries
> in a narrative series I'm doing about a
> family of settlers in twentieth century
> New York, the Glasses. It is a long-term

project, patently an ambitious one, and
there is a real enough danger, I suppose,
that sooner or later I'll bog down, perhaps disappear entirely, in my own methods, locutions, and mannerisms. On the
whole, though, I'm very hopeful. I love
working on these Glass stories, I've been
waiting for them most of my life, and I
think I have fairly decent, monomaniacal
plans to finish them with due care and all
available skill."

The book sold at a fast clip, outpacing *The Catcher
in the Rye*, even as it basked in its acclaim. But the
reviews were harsh, especially about the second story,
"Zooey," which was generally deemed long-winded
and tendentious in its religious musings. Among the
critics: Alfred Kazin, Joan Didion, Mary McCarthy,
Maxwell Geismar, and Warren French.[178] Overall, said
French, *Franny and Zooey* "is not distinguished art
but a self-improvement tract."[179] Geismar was blunter:
"*Zooey* is an interminable, appallingly bad story."[180]

Perhaps the most surprisingly negative verdict came
from John Updike, an early admirer of Salinger's fiction
and a fellow contributor to *The New Yorker*. Writing
in the *New York Times Book Review*, Updike first
explains the stories in his most cogent voice:

"The Franny of 'Franny' and the Franny of 'Zooey' are not the same person. The heroine of 'Franny' is a pretty college girl," passing through an emotional crisis. "She is attempting to find her way out with the help of a religious book, 'The Way of a Pilgrim.' Her surname, Glass, is never mentioned, nor is her brother Zooey.[181]

"The Franny of 'Zooey', on the other hand, is Franny Glass, the youngest of the seven famous Glass children, all of whom have been in turn wondrously brilliant performers on a radio quiz program, 'It's a Wise Child.'"

Later in the review, Updike unleashes his own opinion, reserving his toughest criticism for the second story. "Zooey," he says, "is just too long; there are too many cigarettes, too many goddams, too much verbal ado about not quite enough." Updike also objects to the religious proselytizing, the "vehement editorializing on the obvious."

One estimable critic, the late Janet Malcolm, did weigh in with a very positive, retrospective review of Salinger's oeuvre. Written in 2001, on the fiftieth anniversary of *The Catcher in the Rye*—and forty years after *Franny and Zooey* was published—she singled out "Zooey" for special praise: "Today 'Zooey' is arguably Salinger's masterpiece. Re-reading it and its companion piece 'Franny' is no less rewarding than re-reading *The Great Gatsby*. It remains brilliant."[182]

Yes, that's what she said—right up there with *The Great Gatsby*. Not *The Catcher in the Rye*, which was undeniably Salinger's masterpiece, but "Zooey," a relatively minor story. Normally a very astute critic, Malcolm was in a tiny minority here. Perhaps a minority of one.

A more representative view at the same time came from Louis Menand, then a critic and professor at the City University of New York and now at Harvard. Writing in *The New Yorker*, Salinger's literary home, he minced no words on Salinger's last three stories, starting with "Zooey." After 1955, Menand said:

> "Salinger stopped writing stories in the conventional sense. He seemed to lose interest in fiction as an art form. Perhaps he thought there was something manipulative or inauthentic about literary device and authorial control. His presence began to dissolve into the world of his creation. He let the puppets take over the theater."[183]

And Norman Mailer couldn't resist criticizing his contemporary rival: In a self-serving 1959 book, appropriately called *Advertisements for Myself*, Mailer dismissed Salinger as "no more than the greatest mind ever to stay in prep school."[184] (In the same essay, Mailer disdained other writers, including Saul Bellow: "I cannot take him seriously as a major novelist." Bellow, of course, went on to win a Nobel Prize in Literature, while Mailer stagnated as a novelist.)

●●●

One Glass story has managed to survive with its reputation more or less intact: "Raise High the Roofbeam, Carpenters." It was published in *The New Yorker* in the same year as "Franny" (1955) and well before "Zooey" (1957). Sandwiched between them, it thus delayed the sequel to "Franny," adding to its mystery and, perhaps, its allure.

"Raise High the Roof Beam, Carpenters" was the first Salinger story to treat the Glass siblings as part of a family. With much help from *New Yorker* editor William Shawn, Salinger produced a story that seems to me short on plot or meaning but replete with spot-on dialogue and amusing satire. It is narrated by Buddy, the second oldest of the Glass brothers, who is on army leave to attend the 1942 wedding of Seymour, the oldest, most revered, and most mystical of the Glass siblings.

The unusual title comes not from anything Zen or Christian, but rather from Sappho, an ancient Greek poet: "Raise high the roof beam, carpenters. Like Ares comes the bridegroom, taller far than a tall man."

The Glass family, being an erudite bunch, adopts the slogan after sister Boo Boo scrawls it with soap on a mirror in their apartment, as homage to Seymour before his wedding. Problem is, far from standing tall, Seymour doesn't show up at his own wedding, leaving Muriel, his bride-to-be, stranded at the altar.

What follows is an aimless story, though witty in places. The shocked wedding guests all leave the church to commiserate with the bride's family. Buddy finds himself in a car with four or five of the guests, who proceed to criticize Seymour, while Buddy struggles to defend his absent brother, or at least try to explain him. Since the reader knows from an earlier story, "A Perfect Day for Bananafish," that Seymour later killed himself in 1948, I was hardly surprised that the group decided Seymour needs a psychiatrist. In the end, we learn that Seymour and Muriel later eloped.

When the book version was published eight years later, "Raise High the Roof Beam, Carpenters" drew mostly positive reviews. John Updike called it "a magic and hilarious prose-poem...the best of the Glass pieces,"[185] faint praise perhaps, since he panned "Zooey" in the same review. Orville Prescott of the *New York Times* said: "Its dialogue is expert, its satirical comedy amusing, its style fluid and graceful." But he then expressed frustration with Salinger's meanderings. Salinger is clearly a literary craftsman, he wrote. "But whether there is more than meets the eye in his stories, as is constantly suggested, is a moot point. Could there be less?"[186]

● ● ●

Salinger's next story, "Seymour: An Introduction," was published in the June 6, 1959, issue of *The New Yorker*, again with much help from editor William Shawn. It was packaged as a book four years later along with "Raise High the Roof Beam, Carpenters"—a double-header for Salinger fans.

The story is again narrated by Buddy Glass, conveyor of Salinger's religious beliefs and biases—a fictional clone of his creator. Like Salinger, Buddy once wrote a best-selling novel about a teenager refusing to grow up. Like Salinger, he published two short stories about his older brother, Seymour, one about his wedding, the other about his suicide. And like Salinger, Buddy disdained arrogant academics as "a peerage of tin ears," a marvelous phrase that pinpoints Salinger's envy-cum-hostility over his lack of a college education.

In his telling, Buddy reveals much about the mysterious Seymour. We learn that Seymour was a child prodigy and a college professor at nineteen. We learn that he was a gifted poet. And we learn that he loved Chinese and Japanese poetry, mastering the art of writing Japanese haiku. Above all, Seymour is See More, the embodiment of spirituality, a religious guru delivering God's message via his devoted siblings.

It is hard, however, to imagine Seymour as a vivid character, even a viable person. Because he killed himself years earlier, he speaks only in his diary entries and in letters to his siblings. Missing is the give-and-take of dialogue, so vital to a Salinger story. And his martyrdom may be worthy of a mystical guru, but not of a real person. Seymour becomes an intellectual abstraction, a ghost. I never found him a convincing character.

To make matters worse, Salinger abandoned the linear storytelling that characterized his earlier fiction. Instead, he engages in a kind of post-modernism that has little use for plot or other literary conventions. Buddy just talks and talks, mostly about Seymour's eccentric life, a monologue that Orville Prescott called "intolerably dull"[187] and Irving Howe labeled "hopelessly prolix."[188] As Buddy relates the story of Seymour, he, too, is racked by emotional problems and physical ills.

"Seymour: An Introduction" was widely panned upon publication as a book, with little redeeming value to be found anywhere. It "abandons storytelling altogether" in favor of "unabashed propaganda," wrote critic Warren French in 1963.[189] What propaganda? Only artists, like the poet Seymour, are men of integrity, trying to make their way in an undeserving and imperfect world that does them in.

Many readers saw Seymour as another alter ego for Salinger, his values mirroring Salinger's own. Even Seymour's suicide is manifest in Salinger's retreat to Cornish, where he stops living in this world.

Slawenski put it this way in his 2010 biography, published just after Salinger died: the Glass siblings, especially Seymour, were painted as mystical, even saint-like. Ego, profit, and self-interest were the enemies, spirituality the savior. "The myth of Salinger as an ascetic hermit reluctantly dispensing jewels of enlightenment became indelibly ingrained in the American consciousness," he wrote.[190]

●●●

There's no doubt in my mind that Salinger was in thrall to religious conviction by the mid-1950s. He told his British publisher in 1957 that he had no control over his writing, that God mandated his work. Two years later, he said much the same thing to Judge Learned Hand, his good friend in Cornish: he was driven by deep religious belief, something akin to fatalism, leading him to a feeling that his writing should provide spiritual enlightenment to his readers. As his daughter, Peggy, put it in her memoir:

> "My father once told a friend that...writing was inseparable from the quest for enlightenment, that he intended devoting his life to one great work, and that the work would be his life—there would be no separation."[191]

And that meant seclusion and meditation, which required isolation, reinforcing Salinger's increasingly obsessive quest for privacy. Salinger also came to believe even more deeply that writing was not just a higher calling but, like all art, was deeply spiritual. But if writing was a spiritual undertaking, publishing the result with your name on it represented personal ego, an affront to God, according to his Vedanta religious teachings.

It was a clear conflict, which Salinger ultimately resolved by ceasing to publish anything at all after 1965. Until then, he took it all out on his book publishers, fighting regularly with those profit-mad businessmen who didn't give a fig about the spirituality of his writing.

The great irony, of course, is that the success of Salinger's two books about the Glass family owe more to the public's great interest in their secretive author, which he claimed to abhor, than to any lasting literary merit of the books themselves, spiritual or otherwise.

Salinger never again published great fiction. His last three stories—"Zooey," "Seymour: An Introduction," and "Hapworth 16, 1924" have not aged well. They seem in retrospect little more than a mirror of the religiously obsessed man who wrote them. I can't help thinking: If those stories had been written by John Doe—or anybody not named J. D. Salinger—would they have mattered much? Not likely.

CHAPTER 12

"To See God"

In his spiritual quest, Salinger left no tablet unturned. He explored Buddhism, Hinduism, Ayurveda, Christian Science, and Scientology before settling on Vedanta, a branch of Hinduism. Like ancient Judaism, Vedanta preaches monotheism, including the view that God is ever-present in all things, the ultimate reality. Moreover, each soul is holy, the body just a cover around an inner life centered on God. And Vedanta is ecumenical, meant to coexist with Christianity and Judaism.

To Salinger, Vedanta offered hope that he could conquer the depression that had haunted him off and on since the end of World War II. By developing a personal relationship with God, Salinger embraced the credo: "to see God, to be one with God."

Salinger first learned about Vedanta in 1946, from W. Somerset Maugham's 1944 novel, *The Razor's Edge.* It tells the story of Larry Darrell, an American pilot traumatized by his experience in World War I, including the death of a friend. Rejecting a conventional life, Larry sets off on a search for spiritual meaning, staying for a time in India. There he discovers Eastern religions, including Vedanta, one of six branches of Hinduism. By following its precepts, Larry thrives.

Vedanta, formally known as Advaita Vedanta Hinduism, started in India in ancient times as both a religion and a philosophy, with its ideas written in early Sanskrit texts. Vedanta was brought to the West in 1893 by Swami Vivekenanda, a Calcutta-born monk. Among its many enthusiasts over the years were Leo Tolstoy, William James, Aldous Huxley, Carl Jung, George Santayana, and Henry Miller.[192]

Vedanta's principal text, *The Gospel of Sri Ramakrishna*, is a dense thousand-page treatise, later translated and published by the Ramakrishna-Vivekenanda Center in New York, which happened to be in a townhouse at 17 East 94th Street, just three blocks from the Salinger family apartment on Park Avenue. Vedanta's ecumenical philosophy is evident in the chapel of the Center in New York: on the altar there is a statue of Ramakrishna, but nearby there are icons of Buddha and of the Virgin Mary with the Christ child.[193]

In 1952, Salinger urged Hamish Hamilton, his publisher in London, to pick up the British rights to *The Gospel of Sri Ramakrishna*, calling it "the religious book of the century." Hamilton declined.

Salinger apparently found in Vedanta something consoling that was missing in Zen Buddhism: a personal relationship with God. By the time *The Catcher in the Rye* was published in 1951, Salinger was already studying with his spiritual tutor, Swami Nikhilananda, who had established the Vivekananda Center in New York in 1933 and presided over it until his death in 1973. Salinger was no dilettante, spending many hours on meditation and study. On occasion, he even travelled to the Center's retreat at Thousand Island Park, near the Canadian border, where he stayed in the cottage where Vivekananda lived in the 1890s.

In a 1972 letter to an ailing Nikhilananda, Salinger expressed his gratitude for guiding him out of his "long dark night," referring to his depression.[194]

> "It may be that reading to a devoted group...is all you do now, but I imagine the students who are lucky enough to hear you read from the Gospel would put the matter rather differently. Meaning that I've forgotten many worthy and important things in my life, but I've never forgotten the way you used to read and interpret...up at Thousand Island Park."[195]

Salinger remained true to Vedanta even after Nikhilananda died a year later. In a letter to his successor in 1975, Salinger wrote, "I read a bit from the Gita [a sacred text] every morning before I get out of bed." As he grew older Salinger spent more and more time on his religious pursuits. And after Salinger himself had died, the Vivekananda Center in New York donated to The Morgan Library & Museum more than twenty letters Salinger had written to Swami Nikhilananda and his successor over the years.[196]

•••

Vedanta is complicated, even by the standards of theology. As I came to understand it, Vedanta consists of four stages of life:[197]

- The first stage is the student or apprenticeship phase. The devotee spends much of his time studying the scriptures.

- In the second phase, the householder marries, forms a family, and earns a living. Even in marriage he remains celibate except for procreation.

- Phase three is gradual withdrawal. The person's duty as a householder comes to an end. At this advanced age, he renounces all physical, material, and sexual pleasures, retires from his social and professional life, and leaves his home to dwell in the forest, where he can spend his time in prayers.

- In phase four, a person is totally devoted to God. He has renounced all desires, fears, hopes, duties, and responsibilities. With no worldly ties, he is virtually merged with God.

Salinger, of course, did not adhere to all these practices, most notably the call for celibacy. He had many affairs, especially with much younger women. (See chapter 13). Yet many other Vedantic principles seem evident in his life: The householder phase with Claire, Peggy, and Matt in Cornish. The withdrawal into isolation. The crusade against materialism and ego. The refusal to publish anything he wrote for the last forty-five years of his life. The daily meditation. The frequent letters to Vedanta swamis. The regular visits to the Ramakrishna-Vivekananda Center.

In the context of Vedanta, it's easier to understand Salinger's increasing isolation in Cornish. By withdrawing from society, even to the point of not publishing anything he had written, he was drawing closer to God, engaging with him through constant prayer, eventually merging with him—"becoming one with God." Salinger was quite consciously trying to follow the strictures of a religion he had been studying and practicing for years. He had become a deep believer in Vedanta.

Peggy wrote that her father never would have married Claire if not for the guidance of the Swamis at the Center. And she relates a story her mother told her about a visit she and Salinger made, shortly after their wedding, to a Swami near Washington, DC: On the train home to Cornish that evening, Claire and Jerry made love in their sleeper car. "It was so nice," she told Peggy. "We did not make love very often. The body was evil... I'm certain I became pregnant with you that night."[198]

Vedantic ideas also showed up in his writing after *The Catcher in the Rye*, starting with "Teddy" and "Bananafish" in *Nine Stories* and exploding in the later Glass stories. Salinger even confided to Nikhilananda that he "intentionally left a trail of Vedantic clues throughout his work, from *Franny and Zooey* onward, hoping to entice readers into deeper study."[199]

In "Raise High the Roof Beam, Carpenters," for instance, an entry in Seymour's diary says, "I have been reading a miscellany of Vedanta all day." And in "Hapworth 16, 1924," Salinger's last published story, Seymour as a seven-year-old prodigy bursts into tribute to Vivekananda for two of his books "perfect for the pockets of any average, mobile boys our age...."

In *Nine Stories*, when Teddy says, "All she was doing was pouring God into God," he is voicing Vedanta's stricture: "God is Everywhere."

Similarly, when Zooey says, "There isn't anyone... that isn't Seymour's Fat Lady...don't you know who that Fat Lady is?...It's Christ himself," he's stressing the Vedanta rule: "Each soul is potentially divine."

Problem was, Salinger was becoming less a story-teller and more a didactic dispenser of religious mysticism. Even the language of a Salinger story changed, from Holden's lively vernacular in *The Catcher in the Rye* to a more self-involved voice. Indian scholar Dipti Pattanaik called it a "solipsistic voice." It was a voice, like Buddy's, that was often a monologue, Pattanaik says. Or a voice that confided secrets, as in Seymour's letters. Or a voice offering advice, like Zooey lecturing Franny. Or a self-absorbed voice, as when Buddy talked about the intricacies of writing fiction.[200] Perhaps John Updike said it best in his review of *Franny and Zooey* in the *New York Times Book Review*: Salinger, he wrote, "has clinched our suspicion that a lecturer has usurped the writing stand."[201]

CHAPTER 13

"The Last Minutes of Her Girlhood"

"I almost always write about very young people."

When J. D. Salinger wrote those words for a contributor's note in *Harper's* magazine in April 1949,[202] he defined a credo that ran from his first published story, "The Young Folks" in 1940 to the later Glass stories in the 1950s and 1960s. His fiction is filled with children and adolescents. There's Holden Caulfield, of course, right up there with Huckleberry Finn as runaway teenagers, and Holden's ten-year-old sister, Phoebe. Then there are the very precocious children in *Nine Stories*: Sybil, four; Lionel, four; Teddy, ten; and Esmé, thirteen. And, finally, there is Franny, the youngest of the seven Glass siblings, a college freshman who was nineteen.

Salinger seemed fascinated by young people partly because he saw them as the epitome of innocence, free of the demands of materialism and conformity. At sixteen, Holden Caulfield resists growing up precisely to avoid what he sees as an adult world of depredation, full of those dreaded "phonies."

In cherishing youthful innocence, Salinger also seems to be cherishing the memory that adults have of themselves as youngsters: loving what they once were, or think they were. It's a form of "retroactive narcissism," said Henry Anatole Grunwald, editor of a series of essays about Salinger, published in 1962, and who later became the managing editor of *Time* magazine.[203]

Moreover, most of the children and young people in a Salinger story are precocious, projecting an extraordinary wisdom beyond their years—none more so than Teddy, the ten-year-old boy genius in "Teddy," his namesake tale in *Nine Stories*. Teddy, who talks like a college student, is a parable of religious mysticism, not at all a realistic character. (See chapter 9.)

The Glass siblings, the focus of Salinger's later fiction, never grow into mature adults. By killing himself at thirty-one, Seymour escapes the indignities of aging. As Adam Kirsch put it in an essay in 2019, the centenary of Salinger's birth, Seymour may have been the guru his siblings claimed, but he never grew beyond the "wise child" of his radio quiz show days.[204] And if Salinger continued to write about the Glass siblings during his exile in Cornish, Kirsch speculated, perhaps we'll finally read about Franny and Zooey as adults.

Or not. Just as it's hard to imagine a grown-up Holden Caulfield, I find it hard to conjure a mature Glass sibling.

•••

But there's more to Salinger's focus on young people and their innocence. His fictional women are often of a certain age: puberty or just beyond. In 1945, for example, Whit Burnett's *Story* magazine printed "Elaine," a story about a young woman who seems to have little chance of finding happiness. After a brief sexual encounter, Elaine tries to return to her previous life, but having lost her innocence, she realizes she can't.

Or consider the 1947 story in *Mademoiselle*, "A Young Girl In 1941 with no Waist at All." It describes Ray, based on Salinger, who falls in love with Barbara, a beautiful, intelligent teenager who "is just past the last minutes of her girlhood."[205]

It's a wonderful line that precisely suggests the post-adolescent age Salinger seemed to prefer in his women—not just in his fiction, but in in his life as well. His life was full of love stories between him and young women, often much younger. Claire Douglas was in high school when he first met her and just twenty-two when he, thirty-six, married her. And Colleen O'Neill, his third and last wife, was forty years younger than Salinger.

Salinger's interest in young women was a pattern that started early. In the summer of 1941, Salinger, twenty-two, met Oona O'Neill, daughter of playwright Eugene O'Neill. They were introduced by Salinger's friend Elizabeth Murray. Oona was just fifteen at the time, a student at the exclusive, all-girls Brearley School in New York. A debutant who frequented the Stork Club, Oona was routinely described as "stunningly beautiful," and Salinger quickly fell for her. They went to movies and plays, dined together regularly, and took long walks. He told his friends about her and showed them photographs.[206]

After Salinger was drafted into the army, he moved around from base to base in the US and rarely saw Oona. They did write long letters to each other, but when Oona's mother, Agnes Boulton, moved to Los Angeles with her new husband, Oona declined an offer of admission to Vassar and went with her. Her ambition: to become an actress. She dated other men and her relationship with Salinger slowly ended. When she turned eighteen, Oona married actor Charlie Chaplin, who was fifty-four. They were married for thirty-four years and had eight children.

Salinger was humiliated by Oona's very-public affair with Chaplin and their subsequent marriage. "Salinger never recovered from losing the love of his life," wrote Paul Alexander.[207] Other biographers went even further. David Shields theorized that Salinger's "lifelong obsession with late adolescent girlhood was at least in part an attempt to regain...Oona."[208]

Salinger didn't hide his bitterness over Oona's marriage to Chaplin. In a letter to Elizabeth Murray in 1943, he wrote:

> "I can see them at home evenings. Chaplin squatting grey and nude, atop his chiffonier, swinging his thyroid around his head by his bamboo cane, like a dead rat. Oona in an aquamarine gown, applauding madly from the bathroom...I'm facetious, but I'm sorry. Sorry for anyone with a profile as young and lovely as Oona's."[209]

A few years later, in 1949, when Salinger was thirty, he struck up a conversation with Jean Miller, a fourteen-year-old girl he met at a swimming pool at the Sheraton Hotel in Daytona Beach, Florida. They took walks on the beach for the next several days, with her parents' consent. The two maintained a long platonic friendship for nearly five years, starting with letters back and forth, some sixty of them from Salinger.[210]

"He loved people my age," Miller said years later in an interview with Shane Salerno, a screenwriter and producer, who tracked her down for a 2013 PBS documentary on Salinger and a related book. "He'd instruct me via letter or via phone on my tennis backhand. He didn't want me to be literary. He wanted to talk about my childhood pursuits."[211]

In one long letter, Miller said, he tried explaining Zen to her: [It's] "living in the moment," she quoted him. "It's having direct experience, forgetting your ego... People should work against having ego. Childlike, pure, nothing between you and the experience. That is the way, according to Jerry Salinger, life should be lived."[212]

When she was eighteen, Salinger wrote Miller a letter, dated October 5, 1953, inviting her to visit him in Cornish:

> "You can arrive up here any time you feel like it, bag and baggage, cigarette holder and all and I'll share my homely fare with you..." "It's easy and quick to fly up here...[then] only ten minutes by car... Smith's taxi service, in Windsor, now knows where the hell my house is."[213]

She did visit Salinger in Cornish, staying overnight. "We were friends," she recalled some sixty years later. "We were buddies. Sex didn't come into it."

Until it did. On a weekend together in Montreal a few weeks later, they had sex, at her initiative. "My rite of passage," she called it. Within a few days, the relationship ended. "I had come between him and his work," Miller recalled, "and it was over."[214]

"There is a pattern to Salinger's interest in young women," Salerno wrote, "innocence admired, innocence seduced, innocence abandoned. Salinger is obsessed with girls at the edge of their bloom."[215] Salerno went on to claim in his book and PBS documentary that Salinger maintained his largely reclusive lifestyle mainly because of his pursuit and dating of very young girls.

Therein lies an obvious problem. Doesn't Salinger's sexual interest in young women conflict with Vedanta edicts against sexual pleasure? And if so, as seems evident, how did he manage the conflict between his religious principles and his personal desire? We don't know. There is no record of Salinger ever having said or written anything about the conflict.

•••

After Salinger's divorce from Claire Douglas in 1967, he developed relationships with several other women. His approach was usually to write letters to women who interested him in some way. Many didn't respond, but some did, leading to a correspondence, and often more.

One such liaison is well-known: his affair with Joyce Maynard, a Yale student and writer who just happened to be half-Jewish. It started when Salinger read Maynard's cover story in the April 23, 1972, issue of the *New York Times Magazine*. The article, entitled "An 18-Year-Old Looks Back on Life," described the various social, cultural, and political factors that influenced her generation, leading to a sense of alienation. "Mine is the generation of unfulfilled expectations," she wrote.

The cover featured a demure Yale freshman with blue jeans, scruffy hair, no makeup. It was as if the cover was deliberately designed for Salinger: Joyce Maynard was the very picture of a guileless girl on the verge of becoming a woman.

Sure enough, she soon received a one-page typed letter from Salinger—he the famous writer, she the Yale freshman who had never read *The Catcher in the Rye*. He told her that he, too, was half-Jewish, that he lived in New Hampshire, and that he wanted his letter to remain totally private. He admired her writing, he said with much flattery, and they embarked on a correspondence over the next few months of her freshman year at Yale.

In one letter, Salinger told Maynard in some detail of his interest in homeopathic medicine, and at one point she mentioned she'd come down with a case of poison ivy. Two days later a small package arrived containing a remedy he prepared for her: spotted jewel weed, a late-blooming flower, saturated in vodka. Her poison ivy disappeared.[216]

In another letter, he asked if she's familiar with the word *landsman*. She was. She knew it meant more than just a person from the same place, the same old country. It suggested a kinship, a deep connection of the heart and soul. Jerry told her they were landsmen.[217]

Maynard also wrote that Salinger explained to her how he came up with the name Holden Caulfield: from the names on a movie theater marquee, William Holden and Joan Caulfield. Maynard's version, however, is suspect: Holden Caulfield was first mentioned in a story accepted by *The New Yorker* in 1941, "Am I Banging My Head Against a Wall?" Though it wasn't published in that form, Salinger had written Holden's name in 1941, well before Joan Caulfield's first movie in 1945.[218]

•••

While working at a summer internship in New York after her freshman year, Maynard visited Salinger in Cornish and stayed with him on weekends. Just before the start of her sophomore year, she dropped out of Yale to live with him. She was eighteen, he fifty-three.

Peggy was away at boarding school when Maynard moved in with Salinger. Once, on a trip home, she met Maynard. There they were, two teenagers: One of them, age eighteen, was Jerry's mistress, the other, age sixteen, was "Daddy's" daughter. Here's how Peggy recalled the meeting in her memoir:

> "This is what Daddy has been waiting
> for all this time? I mean she was perfectly
> nice and everything, but who expects
> to find someone looking like a 12-year-
> old-girl. In the place of a potential step-

mother, here was this bizarre little sister
of sorts. It was so *weird*."[219]

Salinger continued his daily routine, retreating every
morning to write and to meditate. His goal in meditating, Maynard wrote, is to obliterate the ego—"nothing
less than to empty his brain of thought...The Zen term
he used for it is *samadhi* or "no mind."[220]

At first, the relationship was loving and supportive,
Maynard said. "Jerry and I established a small tradi-
tion," she wrote. "On Saturday nights...we watch *The
Lawrence Welk Show* together. We dance along with
the music." In retrospect, Maynard admitted that she
naïvely thought the relationship would lead to marriage and children. Within a few months, however,
things soured.

At one point, Maynard and Salinger went to
Daytona Beach for a vacation, bringing Salinger's children, Peggy and Matt, with them. Alone on the beach
with Salinger, Maynard broached the subject of having
her own children. She reported Salinger's response: "I
can never have any more children. I'm finished with
this." He then added: "You better go home now. You
need to clear your things out of my house. If you go
now, you can have everything gone before the children
and I get back. I don't want them upset, having to wit-
ness all this."[221]

Later, according to Maynard, Salinger told Peggy
and Matt that Maynard's father was sick, and she had

to return to New York. He gave her two fifty-dollar bills the next morning and put her in a cab to the airport. The relationship was over, after ten months of living together.

When the relationship ended, Maynard didn't speak or write about her time with Salinger, turning down many such requests. Then, twenty-five years later, in 1998, she published a tell-all memoir called *At Home in the World*, revealing much of their brief life together. For one thing, Maynard was exceptionally frank about her sex life with Salinger. The reader is delicately informed that Maynard had some sort of physical problem that prevented her from having sexual intercourse with Salinger. When Salinger's homeopathic remedies failed to help, they settled for oral sex, with Maynard servicing Salinger. The story of their sex life was repeated a year later by Paul Alexander in *Salinger: A Biography*.

At the end of her memoir, naïve as well as blunt, Maynard confessed how stunned she was to learn that Salinger had written letters to other women, like those she had received: "I felt excommunicated. My letters from J. D. Salinger were my secret treasure, proof of my specialness. It had never occurred to me that some other girl elsewhere might be in possession of letters, too."

Soon after, Maynard auctioned at Sotheby's fourteen letters Salinger had written to her in the early 1970s. The buyer: Peter Norton, a philanthropist and software entrepreneur in California, who paid $156,500, saying he would return the letters to Salinger. They were never made public.[222]

Maynard was roundly criticized for writing about her relationship with Salinger and putting his letters up for sale to the highest bidder. Maureen Dowd, for instance, in a 1999 column for the *New York Times*, called her a "leech woman," a "highly skilled predator," like Monica Lewinsky with President Bill Clinton.[223] On the other hand, novelist Joyce Carol Oates defended Maynard: "...her decision to sell [Salinger's] letters is her own business, like her decision to write about her own life. Why is one 'life' more sacrosanct than another?"[224]

Nearly twenty years later, Maynard wrote her own op-ed column for the *New York Times*,[225] sensibly arguing that if her affair with Salinger had occurred in the Me-Too era of the 2020s, Salinger might have been the one ostracized for his behavior: a fifty-three-year-old celebrity taking advantage of a nineteen-year-old college girl.

●●●

There were other women as well, including Janet Eagleson, a nonfiction writer in Maine with whom he corresponded and bedded in Cornish in 1980 and 1981. A typed, hand-signed letter from him to her dated March 30, 1980, was offered at a Boston auction in 2015, well after Salinger had died.[226]

Sometimes, Salinger went to extraordinary lengths to meet women he saw on TV. One was Catherine Oxenberg, an attractive twentysomething blond featured on *Dynasty*, a popular nighttime soap opera. "Salinger fell in love with her," according to Ian Hamilton, and he flew to Los Angeles to pursue her in 1987.[227] Unannounced, he showed up on the set, said Hamilton, "and he had to be escorted off." The incident was reported by *Spy* magazine in a short item in its December 1987 issue, sparking newspaper stories.[228]

One of the few women Salinger is known to have dated who was not in "the last minutes of her girlhood" was Elaine Joyce, a thirty-six-year-old television actress who appeared in *Green Acres*, *Beverly Hills 90210*, and *Murder, She Wrote*. Salinger, then sixty-two, saw her in a TV series, liked what he saw, and wrote her a letter. "I get fan mail all the time, but I was shocked...It took me forever, but I wrote back...," she told biographer Paul Alexander.[229] "We were involved for a few years all the way through the 1980s. You could say there was a romance." Salinger even went to Jacksonville, Florida, in May 1982 to see Joyce act in a play called 6 *Rms Riv Vu*, one of the few times the press reported on their relationship. Salinger's affair with Elaine Joyce ended in the late 1980s, and she later married playwright Neil Simon.

Salinger soon reverted to form by dating a woman, Colleen O'Neill, who was in her twenties, four decades younger than Salinger. The saga of their relationship is cryptic, not unlike a Salinger short story, and was pieced together by none other than Joyce Maynard, who researched, reported, and wrote a detailed account in her memoir:[230]

> When still in her late teens, Colleen had taken a bus to the Dartmouth Winter Carnival to meet a friend. She struck up a conversation with an older, silver-haired man sitting next to her. When the bus ended its run at White River Junction, she still had to get to Hanover, five miles away, where Dartmouth is located. She asked the man where she might find another bus or a taxi. He offered to drive her to Dartmouth, telling her his name was Jerry Salinger.
>
> Do you mean J. D. Salinger? she asked.
>
> After the drive to Dartmouth, they exchanged addresses and began to correspond. It wasn't a romance, said Phyllis Theroux, a writer who befriended Colleen a couple of years later when she worked as an au pair for the Theroux family. At the time, Colleen, twenty-two, was dating a young man named Mike D., who had a toddler son from a previous relationship. She soon moved to

Pennsylvania, where Mike D. lived. They married, and she adopted Mike Jr. She and Salinger continued to exchange letters from time to time.

Fast forward three years. Colleen abruptly left the marriage with no explanation. Her forwarding address was a post office box in Windsor, Vermont, and she soon filed for divorce. "I wrote to her every day for two years," Mike D. later told Joyce Maynard. "I felt she had some kind of breakdown...I didn't understand what was happening. We were heartbroken."

Mike D. never remarried, but in 1988 Colleen O'Neill, then in her late-twenties, quietly married J. D. Salinger, 69, and lived with him until his death in 2010. Over the years, she occasionally visited Mike Sr. and Mike Jr. and contributed to Mike Jr.'s support.[231]

•••

Though Salinger's lifestyle over the years included several sexual relationships, his fiction did not. There is no sex in a Salinger story, not in *The Catcher in the Rye*, not in the Glass stories, not in his war stories. There is love, but it's usually in a relationship in which sex is ruled out—between brother and sister, for example (Holden and Phoebe or Franny and Zooey), or between mother and child ("Down at the Dinghy"), or between a young woman and her deceased lover ("Uncle Wiggily in Connecticut"). Even when sex is a distinct possibility with other characters, it typically isn't acknowledged, let alone described in any way.

In short, Salinger generally does not depict "mature" love between consenting adults in his fiction. He much preferred to write about children and young adults, especially women in the last minutes of their girlhood. For Salinger, they remained childlike in their innocence—just the way he wanted them.

CHAPTER 14

Sightings and Skirmishes

Though he insisted on maintaining his privacy in Cornish, New Hampshire for more than fifty years, Salinger often came out of hiding. He vacationed in Florida nearly every winter, first with Claire and the children, usually in a non-descript motel and often under assumed names. Later, he went to Florida alone or with his latest love interest. He also travelled to New York quite regularly, sometimes to visit editor William Shawn at *The New Yorker*, or to meet with John Keenan, his wartime buddy who became a New York policeman. While in the city, he usually dropped by the Gotham Book Mart, then a famous bookstore and literary hangout on West 47th Street, to browse the shelves and chat with its proprietor, Andreas Brown.

Once in a while, he would bring Peggy along when he went to see Shawn, who was Peggy's godfather. She had met him several times before, but only once at his office. "Even though I was only seven," Peggy later wrote in her memoir, "Mr. Shawn stood up, as though he were in the presence of a young lady, shook my hand, and offered me a seat." She then played in the magazine's art department before going to lunch at the Algonquin, the famous watering hole of *New Yorker* staffers, Broadway actors, and assorted celebrities— hardly the lunch venue for a reclusive writer. They were joined by Shawn and Lillian Ross, a writer for the magazine and Shawn's paramour. Ross later wrote Peggy a charming note, signed "Love, Lillian."[232]

Salinger even met with a television director named Peter Tewksbury, who wanted to create a film version of "For Esmé—With Love and Squalor." The two men exchanged script ideas by mail for three months, but Salinger rejected any changes to his original story. They soon dropped the idea.[233]

But it's surprising that Salinger, averse to publicity or displays of ego, showed any interest at all. He had sworn off Hollywood years earlier, after a bad experience in 1949 when Samuel Goldwyn made a movie out of "Uncle Wiggily in Connecticut." Called *My Foolish Heart*, it starred Dana Andrews and Susan Hayward and deviated greatly from Salinger's short story. The screenplay was especially weak, a major surprise because it was written by Julius and Philip Epstein, the twin brothers who had scripted the brilliant *Casablanca* just a few years earlier. "Wrong story, wrong producer, wrong cast," Salinger wrote in a letter to Elizabeth Murray, "but I paid a lot of bills with the money."[234] Even Goldwyn's biographer, A. Scott Berg, called *My*

Foolish Heart a "bastardization" of "Uncle Wiggily in Connecticut."

The experience stayed with Salinger for more than fifty years. Near the end of his life, he created the J. D. Literary Trust to manage his published and unpublished work. The Trust explicitly stated that *The Catcher in the Rye* could never be turned into a film. And it hasn't. Nor has any other Salinger story.

●●●

As Salinger's fame soared in the early 1960s, several reporters tried to ferret him out in his own backyard. One of the first was *Newsweek*'s Mel Elfin, who attempted to pierce what he called Salinger's "iron curtain." On a trip to Cornish in 1960, Elfin talked to everyone who would talk: the mailman, a few shopkeepers, and the local librarian, who kept *Catcher* on the restricted shelf. He drove to Dartmouth, where he learned that Salinger "frequently uses the facilities of the Baker Memorial Library."[235] Elfin reported that Salinger was a registered Republican, chain-smoked cigarettes, and sometimes attended town meetings with Claire. And Salinger's neighbor, Bernard Yeaton, told Elfin that Salinger routinely rose by 6:00 AM or so, then "walked down the hill to his studio, a tiny concrete shelter with a translucent plastic roof." (See page 105.) Elfin was the first journalist to disclose such details.

A few months later, *Time* magazine one-upped *Newsweek* by putting Salinger on its cover—a milestone moment that anointed Salinger as more than a cult figure who had written an iconic novel nearly a decade earlier.[236] Though Salinger hated the *Time* story and deplored the attention it brought, there was no denying he was a literary star, a major figure worthy of a *Time* cover, whose subject a week earlier was Nikita Khrushchev. He had become a "celebrity recluse," an apt oxymoron that described his unique status.

Time's piece, called "Sonny, an Introduction," was pegged to the 1961 release of *Franny and Zooey*, a book version of the two stories that had run years earlier in *The New Yorker*. It added a few details to Elfin's pioneering piece in *Newsweek*, tracking down Salinger's sister, Doris, a buyer at Bloomingdale's. "Why don't you just leave us alone," she complained. But neither *Newsweek* nor *Time* mentioned Salinger's growing obsession with young women or his religious interest in Vedanta.

Less than two months later, *Life* magazine, a sister publication of *Time*, followed with a nine-page spread of text and photos. A *Life* photographer managed to snap a surreptitious photo of Salinger that defined his image for years to come: gaunt and unsmiling, with graying hair, leaning on a cane, and wearing a one-piece jumpsuit. *Life* also ran a shot of the Salinger family dog peering out under the fence around the house. The writer of the piece, Ernest Havemann, briefly encountered Salinger's wife, Claire:

> "A young woman with blondish hair, barefoot and without makeup, stood there holding her startled baby...Behind her was a little girl who had a friendly and expectant look, as if she hoped I had brought her a playmate..." After Havemann told her he was a journalist, "Mrs. Salinger's eyes said unmistakably, 'Oh, Lord, not another one.'"[237]

Then there was Edward Kosner.[238] Though he never visited Cornish, he added a few more nuggets to the Salinger saga in the *New York Post Magazine*.[239] He told of a college student who worked as a night office boy at *The New Yorker* and encountered Salinger on several evenings when he was working on "Seymour: An Introduction." Here's his recollection of Salinger:

> "...There'd be just the two of us in this big, dark building...He was writing seven days a week...But he was never too busy to stop, light a cigarette and have a cup of coffee and talk to me...He *listens*. I was very mixed up at the time...and he helped me a lot. I'm very grateful to him."

● ● ●

Salinger often sacrificed his privacy to do battle with people threatening his interests, especially his literary rights. In the fall of 1974, for example, Salinger received a tip from Andreas Brown of the Gotham Book Mart: someone calling himself "John Greenberg from Berkeley, California" was peddling a pirated edition of a collection of Salinger's short stories. The two-book paperback set contained twenty-three short stories, most of which Salinger had published between 1940 and 1948 in various magazines, including *Collier's*, the *Saturday Evening Post*, and *Esquire*. But the stories had never been collected in an anthology.[240]

The illegal paperbacks, a clear violation of Salinger's copyright, were called *The Complete Uncollected Short Stories of J. D. Salinger: Vols. 1 and 2*. The stories had been obtained from various libraries that had copies of them. Book wholesalers, all using the name "John Greenberg from Berkeley, California" were selling the books to retailers in several cities, from San Francisco to New York. Within two months, about twenty-five thousand copies of these books, priced at three to five dollars for each volume, had been sold around the country.

Salinger was so angered by the theft of his work that he filed a civil suit in Federal District Court in San Francisco, asking for a sales injunction against seventeen major bookstores and seeking $250,000 in punitive damages from "John Greenberg."

Salinger went even further, making a rare call to a reporter to publicize his case. The lucky journalist was Lacey Fosburgh, a San Francisco-based staffer for the *New York Times*. Salinger told her that he wrote the stories long ago and never intended to publish them. "I wanted them to die a perfectly natural death," he told Fosburgh in a near-half-hour phone call from Cornish. Then in a statement that spoke volumes about himself, he said:

> "There is a marvelous peace in not publishing. It's peaceful...Publishing is a terrible invasion of my privacy. I like to write. I live to write. But I write just for myself and my own pleasure."[241]

When Fosburgh asked whether he intended to publish again, Salinger demurred, saying he was not under contract with anyone to publish anything and didn't "necessarily intend to publish posthumously."

"I pay for this kind of attitude," Salinger added. "I'm known as a strange, aloof kind of man. But all I'm doing is trying to protect myself and my work."

Fosburgh's story, "J. D. Salinger Speaks About His Silence," ran on the front page of the *New York Times* on November 3, 1974. The bookstores were enjoined from any further sales of the unauthorized paperbacks, but "John Greenberg" wasn't found.

Nearly fifty years later, it's possible to buy the two original, pirated books online, no questions asked. I recently found that Amazon offered a few copies from independent booksellers at prices that often topped $1,000 for the two-book paperback set, and eBay has listed a couple of auctions of one or both volumes, the price depending on the bidding. In the interests of full disclosure, I bought both books, via Amazon, from a bookstore in Cincinnati called Von's Shops. The price: $595, plus tax. The paperback books are slender with small, hard-to-read type. Still, it's the simplest way, if not the cheapest, to read Salinger's early stories. They are not easy to find.

•••

The *New York Times* story spurred even more media interest. *Newsweek* again sent a reporter, Bill Roeder this time, to try to interview Salinger in Cornish. And he managed to catch a glimpse—when Salinger himself opened the door after Roeder knocked.

"Salinger, tall, gaunt, and gray-haired at 55, was dressed in a blue jump suit," Roeder wrote in *Newsweek*'s November 18, 1974, issue. Roeder introduced himself, then asked Salinger whether he was still writing.

"Of course I'm writing," Salinger replied.

Roeder asked about his life in Cornish.

"I like to hang on to my privacy—my undocumented privacy."

Then Salinger added: "Is there anything more boring than a talking writer?"

After a few minutes, Roeder decided to end the awkward conversation, which he recognized was unfairly intrusive. He extended his hand to offer thanks for the chat and to say goodbye. Salinger extended his own hand, saying, "This is not a friendly gesture. I really don't appreciate your coming here."

Other reporters stalked Salinger, managing brief conversations that were turned into newspaper stories. There was Michael Clarkson from the *Niagara Falls Review*, who showed up in Salinger's driveway one day in 1978.[242] And Betty Eppes from the *Baton Rouge Advocate* who arranged a meeting with Salinger in 1981 outside a store in Windsor, Vermont, just across the covered bridge from Cornish.[243]

I have never understood why Salinger agreed to meet Eppes, but he talked to her for half an hour or so, saying little of any substance. What he didn't know was that Eppes had hidden a tape recorder in the sleeve of her blouse, capturing twenty-seven minutes of their conversation. Eppes wrote a story for her newspaper, and then published a more detailed account in the *Paris Review*, Summer 1981 issue. The tape, Eppes has since said, is locked away in a safety deposit box, and she has vowed never to release it. "I came to regret it," Eppes said in 2021. "Sometimes...I think I stole his voice... That tape is not mine to give or sell."[244]

Then there were the paparazzi who stalked Salinger until they got a photograph or two—including freelancers Paul Adao and Steve Connolly, who double-teamed Salinger outside a supermarket, snapping a photo that made it onto the front page of the *New York Post* in April 1988.[245]

● ● ●

In 1986, Salinger went to court again, this time in a far more significant case than the pirated paperbacks. He tried to stop Random House from publishing a biography called *J. D. Salinger: A Writing Life*, by Ian Hamilton, a distinguished British literary critic who had previously written a well-regarded biography of poet Robert Lowell. Salinger's complaint: Hamilton had quoted, without permission, from letters Salinger had written to friends over the years, including Whit Burnett, Elizabeth Murray, Learned Hand, and even one to Ernest Hemingway.

The letters, eighty to one hundred of them, had never been published, but Hamilton tracked most of them down. In one instance, he received some thirty letters directly from Jamie Hamilton, Salinger's onetime publisher in Britain. Salinger had written the letters to Jamie and his deputy, Roger Machell, over a ten-year period, starting in 1951, the year *Catcher* was published. The letters were not mere copies, but rather the yellowing originals. According to Ian Hamilton, the letters gave Salinger's response to the reviews of *The Catcher in the Rye* and his take on John Woodburn, who edited *Catcher* and *Nine Stories* at Little, Brown. Ian Hamilton obtained even more Salinger letters from various universities. Harvard Law School, for instance, gave him copies of all thirteen letters Salinger had written to Judge Learned Hand from 1955 to 1961. Princeton did the same for the large number of letters, including those dating to World War II from Salinger to Whit Burnett, his early mentor at *Story* magazine. And the University of Texas allowed Hamilton to read all thirty-eight of Salinger's letters to his longtime friend, Elizabeth Murray.

It was a treasure trove, and Ian Hamilton claimed he could quote from any of the letters in a limited way under the doctrine of "fair use."[246]

The legal case posed two related and very basic questions: Is the reading public entitled to know what a famous writer, clearly a public figure, says in his own words about a matter of public interest? Or does a public figure like Salinger have the right of privacy when it comes to his unpublished letters?

Ian Hamilton had originally written to Salinger in 1983 telling him of his plans to write a biography of his "life and work" to be published by Random House, and to ask for an opportunity to talk to Salinger. Hamilton knew full well that others had made similar requests over the years, to no avail, and that he wouldn't fare any better. But he had to try.

A few weeks later, Salinger replied, a surprise in itself, but with the expected message. His letter of rejection showed just why Hamilton was so eager to quote from Salinger's other letters over the years, to capture the tone and style of Salinger's writing. His letter is worth quoting in full:

> *Dear Sir:*
>
> *You say you've been commissioned by Random House to write a book about me and my work (you put it, perhaps undeliberately, in just that order), and I have no good reason to doubt your word, I'm exceedingly sorry to say. I might just add, probably not at all wisely, that it has always been a most terrible and almost unassailable wonder to me that it is evidently quite lawful, the world over, for a newspaper or publishing house to "commission" somebody, in the not particularly fair name of good journalism or basic profitable academic research, to break into the privacy not only of a person not reasonably suspected of criminal activity but into the lives as well, however glancingly, of that person's relatives and friends. I've despaired long ago of finding any justice in the common practice. Let alone any goodness or decency.*

Speaking (as you may have gathered)
from rather unspeakably bitter expe-
rience, I suppose I can't put you or
Random House off because the lot of you
are determined to have your way, but I
do feel I must tell you, for what very little
it may be worth, that I think I've borne
all the exploitation and loss of privacy I
can possibly bear in a single lifetime.

Sincerely yours,
J. D. Salinger[247]

Hamilton, of course, wrote his book anyway, sub-
mitting the manuscript to Random House in July 1985.
In the normal vetting process, Random House lawyers
saw that Hamilton had quoted extensively from doz-
ens of Salinger's unpublished letters, but the lawyers
deemed it acceptable "fair use," partly because many
of the excerpts were relatively brief. Random House
then produced about sixty-five bound galleys of the
book in 1986 to be sent to book reviewers and others. A similar process played out in England, where
Heinemann, a well-known publishing company, was
set to release the book, with the *Observer* newspaper
slated to run excerpts. The book was set in type, a book
jacket designed, and bound galleys sent to reviewers. So
far, so good.

Then, on May 25, 1986, Random House received a letter from the New York law firm of Kay Collyer & Boose, on behalf of J. D. Salinger. He had read the bound galleys of Hamilton's book, the law firm said, and wanted all quotations from his unpublished letters removed. Otherwise, he would take all necessary legal steps to have the book enjoined from publication.

Though they felt on safe legal ground, lawyers at Random House asked Hamilton to reduce the number and length of any direct quotes from the unpublished Salinger letters—perhaps in the hope of placating Salinger, as well as reducing the risk of running afoul of the fair use rules in any subsequent litigation. Hamilton complied, cutting some quotes and paraphrasing others. Ultimately, there were only about two hundred of Salinger's words in a manuscript of more than thirty thousand words.

It wasn't good enough. Salinger decided to proceed with his lawsuit. His affidavit said he was "utterly dismayed" to discover the "core" of Hamilton's book was "in my own words." He accused Hamilton of using his literary property to "flesh out an otherwise lifeless and uninteresting biography." After some more skirmishing, both Salinger and Hamilton were required to give in-person depositions and be interrogated by lawyers for the other side. In other words, Salinger would have to show up in court and answer questions for hours. The reclusive author, now sixty-seven, would have to go public to protect his privacy.

On October 10, 1986, Salinger came to New York—to the midtown law offices of Satterlee & Stephens, whose lawyer, Robert Callagy, was representing Hamilton and Random House. The process lasted six hours, starting at 2:00 PM. At one point, Salinger turned to his lawyer, Marcia Paul, to ask: "Do I really have to answer all these questions?"

Salinger was so nervous that he had asked Lillian Ross to accompany him to the proceedings. "He would come over to my place and wait until we'd have to go, and I'd go with him," Ross later told Andreas Brown of the Gotham Book Mart. "Literally, sometimes I'd have to hold his hands he was shaking so badly. Afterwards I'd make him chicken soup at the end of the day. He was...a fragile person, so vulnerable to the world."[248]

A month later, the verdict came in the US District Court in New York: Judge Pierre Leval issued a thirty-page ruling in favor of Hamilton. He could publish his book, including the excerpts from Salinger's unpublished letters. "Although [Salinger's] desire for privacy is surely entitled to respect," Judge Leval wrote, "as a legal matter it does not override a lawful undertaking to write about him using legally available resources... Hamilton's book cannot be dismissed as...snooping into a private being's private life for commercial gain. It is a serious, well-researched history of a man who through his own literary accomplishments had become a figure of enormous public interest. This favors a finding of fair use."

Salinger's side filed an immediate appeal to the US Court of Appeals for the Second Circuit in New York. On January 29, 1987, Judges Jon Newman and Roger Miner reversed Judge Leval's ruling, granting Salinger a preliminary injunction against publication of Hamilton's book. Why? For one thing, they said that Hamilton's paraphrasing of Salinger's words too closely tracked the original, depriving Salinger of copyright protection. For another, they claimed that Salinger's letters deserved protection because they were private missives that had not been previously published.

In the clash between Salinger's right to privacy and the public's right to know, privacy won. Or as Hamilton put it, "The Newman-Miner verdict had brought the Copyright Act into direct collision with the First Amendment."

But if privacy was Salinger's goal, I don't think he really won. In covering the case, the *New York Times* quoted freely from Salinger's original letters in the bound galleys—far more than Hamilton did in his revised manuscript. One such letter criticized Wendell Willkie, the 1940 presidential candidate seeking to dethrone FDR. Salinger wrote that Willkie, "looks to me like a guy who makes his wife keep a scrapbook for him."[249]

Other periodicals, from the *Times Literary Supplement* in Britain to *New York Magazine*, did the same. Moreover, as part of his lawsuit, Salinger was required to file all the disputed letters at the Copyright

Office in Washington, where anyone willing to pay ten dollars could read the letters.

Undeterred by his loss in the Second Circuit, Hamilton took the case to the Supreme Court, with significant support from other publishers, journalists, and historians. As one publisher speculated, what if "a news reporter discovers Oliver North's private diary, but can neither quote nor paraphrase from it because it is unpublished?"[250]

But the Supreme Court didn't show a shred of interest. On October 5, 1987, it declined to hear the case, without offering any explanation. The Second Circuit court ruling remained in force, and Hamilton had to rewrite his book without quoting or paraphrasing anything from the Salinger letters. Hamilton's stripped-down book, *In Search of J. D. Salinger*, was published in 1988. The 222-page book was informative in many ways, but largely lacking Salinger's unique voice, it was a bit like reading *Hamlet* without the soliloquies.

And what of Hamilton's original book, *J. D. Salinger: A Writing Life*? Only sixty-five copies of the bound galleys with the extensive material from Salinger's letters were distributed in 1986 in the US. I recently purchased one such copy from Jeff Hirsch Books, a dealer in Wadsworth, Illinois, and I feel lucky to have it. Yet I'm saddened that others can't easily read what Hamilton wanted to say using Salinger's own words. It's a far better book than the one that Hamilton was allowed to publish two years later.

Father Figure

J. D. Salinger had two children, both with his second wife, Claire Douglas, and they couldn't have been more different in how they viewed their father.

Margaret Salinger, known as Peggy ever since her birth on September 10, 1955, wrote a sometimes-blistering memoir, *Dream Catcher*, in 2000, which painted her father as cold, manipulative, abusive, and, well, just weird: he drank his own urine, she wrote, and sat in an orgone box, a closet-sized cabinet said to store psychic energy, especially sexual energy.[251] Peggy claims her mother was so unhappy in her marriage that she considered suicide.[252]

Matthew Salinger, four years younger than Peggy, immediately jumped to his father's defense, dismissing her memoir as "gothic tales of our supposed childhood."[253] In a letter to the *New York Observer*, he wrote, "I would hate to think I were responsible for her book selling one single extra copy, but...I just know that I grew up in a much different house, with two different parents than my sister described."[254] To the *Sunday*

Times of London, he said in 2000, "I guess she's got a lot of anger. But to write a book just isn't right."[255]

Peggy thought otherwise. After her son was born, she felt an "urgency" to air the family's dirty laundry, she said, in order to come to terms with her troubled relationship with her father. To undergo the catharsis she sought, she decided that writing a book was the best course.

Dream Catcher is the disturbing result. At more than four hundred pages, it is full of her own recollections, as well as details of her father's early life gleaned from her aunt Doris (Salinger's sister) and from her mother (Salinger's ex-wife, Claire).

It's not all bleak, not all a "strife-with-father" memoir, as one reviewer put it. Peggy has many happy, early memories of "Daddy," when he was "funny, intensively loving, and the person you most want to be with." Her memoir contains photos of Peggy as a toddler with her beaming young father. "The world just lit up when Daddy came home."[256]

Peggy's early years with Daddy were often close. He rarely read books to her—that was Claire's role—but he loved showing her his collection of reel-to-reel movies. In those pre-cassette days, he would set up the screen in front of the fireplace, and she would lie on the floor. She watched him take the reel from its round metal case, place it on the sprocket of the film projector, then thread the film through the projector to the empty reel at the back of the projector. What did they watch together? A lot of Hitchcock movies, Laurel and Hardy, W. C. Fields, the Marx Brothers. And musicals, including his favorite, *Gigi*, about a young girl being groomed as a courtesan. To this day, Peggy wrote in her memoir, "I can still sing the lyrics" from *Gigi*, especially "The Night They Invented Champagne."[257]

Peggy regularly went with her father on his daily trips to the post office in Windsor, Vermont, and she often walked along the wooded path to his writing bunker to bring him his lunch. She frequently accompanied him on trips to New York, visiting various Holden Caulfield landmarks.

When Peggy was eight, President John F. Kennedy was assassinated, and sadness gripped the Salinger household, as it did in families across America. "The only time I have ever seen my father cry in my whole life was the day he watched JFK's funeral procession on television," she recalled in her memoir.[258] Just a year earlier, Salinger had turned down an invitation to a dinner at the White House, even though Jackie Kennedy had personally called him on the phone to urge him to attend.

Salinger often expressed his love for his young children. After his separation from Claire, he took Peggy, eleven, and Matt, seven, to New York to see the sights, staying at the Drake Hotel. One evening, while he was reading in bed, he stopped to look at his children asleep nearby. "I loved...watching their sleeping bodies in the same room," he wrote to Michael Mitchell, a close friend who had designed the cover for *The Catcher in the Rye.* "I love going anywhere with them."[259]

Years later, in a letter to Matt, he wrote, "I can't say I cared much for the War or military school, or my childhood. These Cornish years with you and Peggy and this house...and my notebooks and work...and our trips to London and Lake Placid and Dublin and Montreal and Andover—these years are what I would call my real life."[260]

Nostalgia? Perhaps. A desire to remember the rosy side of his earlier life? Maybe. But Salinger was, by many accounts, a devoted father to his children, especially when they were young. After his divorce, he moved across the street to a new house he had built and saw Peggy and Matt nearly every day, certainly no less than when he had been holed up in his writing bunker for hours on end while married to Claire. And he took them on frequent trips, sometimes together, but usually separately.

When her parents divorced in 1967, the twelve-year-old Peggy went to boarding school, and life got tougher. She became pregnant while still in high school in Lexington, Massachusetts. She and her boyfriend, Dan, a Dartmouth student, agreed on an abortion. "I took, without asking, $150 from my brother's passbook for bus fare to New York and an abortion."[261]

Peggy graduated from high school in 1973 but was rejected for admission by Dartmouth. She then enrolled at New England College in New Hampshire, the nearest school to Dan at Dartmouth. When Peggy was nineteen, their relationship ended. She took up with her karate instructor, impulsively married him, and dropped out of college.

Peggy worked at odd jobs, very odd jobs. She was an airport security guard, a waitress, and then trained to be an auto and truck mechanic at Boston Edison, the local utility, where she worked from 1975 to 1980. While at Boston Edison she took courses at the extension divisions of both Harvard and Boston University. She did well. Encouraged by her supervisor at the utility, she applied to Brandeis University's special program for older students—she was twenty-five—and was accepted as a fulltime student. Her father, after much argument, reluctantly agreed to pay the tuition, though not her living expenses. Soon after, her husband, the former karate instructor, walked out one day, draining their joint bank account.

Fortunately, she loved Brandeis, and Brandeis loved her back. She graduated *summa cum laude*, winning a Phi Beta Kappa key. She also won a fellowship to Oxford University's Centre for Management Studies. And for good measure, her maternal grandmother, Claire's mother, left her a financial stipend that more than covered her education. She was largely freed from begging Daddy for money.

Her painful odyssey from Cornish—the alcoholism, the teenage abortion, the failed marriage—seemed behind her. When she graduated from Oxford in

1985, her mother and brother came to the ceremony. Not Daddy.

Unfortunately, her long string of troubles did not end. Back in the US after Oxford, she had a bladder infection that required surgery at Massachusetts General Hospital. Her father came to see her. "You shouldn't have to go into surgery alone," she remembers him saying.[262] Later, though, when she had yet another health problem, Daddy reverted to his Christian Science belief that illness was a mental illusion, not a disease-based reality. To buttress his argument, he sent her a book, *Science and Health with Key to the Scriptures*, by Mary Baker Eddy, founder of the Christian Science Church. The book's message: you'll get better when you stop believing in the "illusion" of your sickness.

She soon recovered. With her Oxford pedigree, Peggy had no trouble finding jobs in industrial relations, but the work left her unsatisfied. Once again she jumped far afield, like the auto mechanic who went to Oxford. This time she enrolled at the Harvard Divinity School—not with the goal of becoming an ordained minister, but rather with the training needed to counsel needy people.

Along the way, she resumed her interest in singing, and she was good enough to sing in the choir of the Boston Symphony Orchestra. She met and married a former opera singer named Larry, no last name given in her memoir, and had a son, no first or last name offered. At forty-four, she professed great happiness.

And there, in 2000, her memoir ends, except for a final summing up of a lifetime of trying to win the affection of a hard-to-please father.

Her ultimate verdict on J. D. Salinger is harsh. When she was about to give birth to her son, for instance, Peggy was hospitalized for acute septicemia and dehydration. After she returned home with Larry, her father asked, in his one phone call, how she was planning to support her child financially. As Peggy tells it, her answer didn't satisfy him, and, she said, "he attacked me with the impersonal viciousness of an earthquake."[263] He told her she had no right to bring a child she couldn't support into this "lousy" world, adding that he hoped she was considering an abortion.

What followed was an extraordinary exchange that Peggy says she wrote down "verbatim" after the call ended.[264]

"No, Daddy," she remembers saying, "any *normal* parent would offer support. All you offer is criticism."

"I've never criticized you," Salinger responded... "I've always been there for you when you needed it."

"That's absolute crap. You've never once inconvenienced yourself for your children. You've never interrupted your precious work. You've always done exactly what you wanted, when you wanted..."

"...Christ, you're sounding just like every other woman in my life, my sister, my ex-wives. They all accuse me of neglecting them."

"Well, if the shoe fits, wear it."

"I can be accused of a certain detachment, that's all. Never neglect. You just need someone to hate. You always did. First it was your brother, then it was your mother, now it's me. You're still seeing a psychiatrist, aren't you?"

"What does that have to do with anything?"

"You *are*, aren't you. You're not happy with anything. You're nothing but a neurotic malcontent."

And so it went. Peggy called her mother to tell her what happened. Claire, according to Peggy, said "the same thing happened to me when I became pregnant."

Peggy's book ends with a full denunciation of her father, including his fear of mature women, his embrace of "religious abracadabra"[265] and even his fiction. By "conflating aesthetics and theology," she wrote, he transformed his work from "secular fiction" to "hagiography," even granting sainthood to Seymour.

Salinger never publicly responded to any of this, and Peggy's memoir remains a one-sided version of a complex father-daughter relationship. The reader, very much including me, longs for Salinger's side of the story: perhaps how an exasperated father tried to cope with a daughter who was a teenage alcoholic, had an abortion in high school, suffered from a bewildering array of illnesses, and married the wrong man. Even when she finally appeared to straighten herself out, she chose not to seek reconciliation but to write a tell-all book attacking her father.

Why? Peggy saw her book as a personal cathar-sis. She told Linton Weeks, who reviewed the book in the *Washington Post* in 2000, that she needed to put her life in perspective. "I now understand what I feel I need to understand...I'm not playing by [his] rules anymore."[266]

However much writing *Dream Catcher* may have helped Peggy cope with her demons, it is a sad book, a literary *tristesse*. There's no hopeful ending, as in "For Esmé—with Love and Squalor." Instead, there's the despair of a father-daughter relationship gone hopelessly wrong. It feels more like "A Perfect Day for Bananafish" or "Teddy," both of which ended in sui-cide. Peggy chose estrangement. She and her father never again spoke to each other.

It didn't help matters that Peggy's book echoed sim-ilar charges against Salinger that Joyce Maynard lev-eled in her memoir published two years earlier. In 1972, when she was just eighteen, Maynard had dropped out of Yale to move in with the fifty-three-year-old Salinger in Cornish. Their affair lasted ten months until Salinger told her to leave. In her book, written twenty-five years later, Salinger is depicted as two different men—loving and considerate early on, and nasty and duplicitous as the relationship soured.

• • •

All of this put Matt Salinger in a difficult position, especially over Peggy's attack on their father. Since Salinger remained his silent self, Matt stepped forward to defend him, citing his own close relationship with the famous father who to him was just Dad.

Matt, born on February 13, 1960, was four years younger than Peggy, and in some ways was like an only child, especially after Peggy left for boarding school when he was seven. After his parents were divorced in 1967, Matt shuttled between their two houses in Cornish, remaining close to both of them. "I was not the child of split parents," he said in 1983. "I got to know my parents as individuals. They became friends to me."[267] He went to Broadway shows with his father, as well as to Dartmouth football games in Hanover. He took horseback riding lessons and played tennis. More easygoing than Peggy, Matt and his father seemed to get along well without the mutual rancor that later plagued the Peggy/Daddy relationship.

As a child, Matt didn't hear much about his father's work. "We were more likely to talk about the Dartmouth football team or what we're going to do when I pick you up on Wednesday," he told *The Guardian* in 2019. In the same interview, he did acknowledge how constantly Salinger thought about his writing. "He teemed with ideas...He'd be driving his car and he'd pull over to write something and laugh to himself. Sometimes he'd read it to me, sometimes he wouldn't. At home, next to every chair he had a notebook."[268]

Unlike Claire and Peggy, Matt was better able to accept his father's long hours in his writing bunker. His desire for privacy, Matt said, "was what he needed for his work, and his work was everything to him."[269]

Despite his father's professed hostility to anything reeking of Ivy League elitism, Matt was white shoe all the way: Andover, where he was a classmate of John F. Kennedy, Jr.; Princeton, where he stayed for a year; and Columbia, where he received his BA degree in art history and drama in 1983.

Why did he leave Princeton? He found it "stifling," he said. "People knew all about everyone else. I didn't want that." Columbia, a much larger university in a big city, afforded him the privacy he craved. "It was wonderful. I was completely anonymous."[270]

After graduating from Columbia, he headed to Hollywood to pursue an acting career, a dream his father once had for himself. Matt achieved considerable success. He acted in or produced sixteen films from 1984 to 2021, including *Captain America*, a 1990 superhero movie in which he played Captain America. He also acted in eight television productions and produced an off-Broadway play in 2000, *The Syringa Tree*, which won several awards, including a Drama Desk Award and an Obie Award for best play of the year. His father came to opening night.

His mother, Claire, moved to California to set up her Jungian psychology practice, largely to be near Matt, his wife, Betsy Jane Becker, and their twin sons born in 1994. He remained close to both parents. He also stayed in occasional touch with Peggy. "I only wish her happiness," he told the *Guardian* in 2019.

These days, Matt, who now lives in Connecticut, spends much of his time sorting through all the writing J. D. Salinger did since he last published anything in 1965. The goal: to release the stories to the public as soon as possible. He never responded to my request for an interview.

Peggy has no role in preparing her father's unpublished work for future release. She was conspicuously excluded from the J. D. Salinger Literary Trust, set up by her father, now run by her brother and her stepmother, Colleen O'Neill Salinger. Punishment, it seems, for her apostasy.

CHAPTER 16

Salinger's Legacy

*"What really knocks me out is a book
that, when you're all done reading it, you
wish the author that wrote it was a terrific
friend of yours and you could call him up
on the phone whenever you felt like."*

—Holden Caulfield, *The Catcher in the Rye*

As he grew old, Salinger remained mentally engaged,
but he was frail and nearly deaf from the injury he
first suffered during World War II. He died on January
27, 2010, at age ninety-one. His death was front-
page news across the country and much of the world.
Television programs chronicled his life, featuring literary critics who analyzed his writing. The internet burst
with tributes, and his four books sold out on Amazon,
bestsellers once again. In the end, Salinger, that great
recluse, was showered with the overwhelming publicity
he had long tried to avoid.

Perhaps Matt Salinger said it best in a statement he
prepared on behalf of the family:

"Salinger had remarked that he was in
this world but not of it. His body is gone
but the family hopes that he is still with
those he loves, whether they are religious
or historical figures, personal friends or
fictional characters."[271]

By choosing a reference to Vedanta that Salinger
loved ("in this world but not of it"), the family rein-
forced his views about an afterlife and the affinity of his
fiction to his own spirituality. But how will he be remembered by the rest of us? What legacy does he leave?

• • •

Even in retrospect, Salinger is not easy to understand, a
man of many contradictions: Passionate yet detached.
Raised Jewish, but a practitioner of mystical Hinduism.
No sex in his books, but plenty in his life. A great
believer in the power of love, but not so ready to give
it. An adult with sophisticated views, but a man of
arrested development in his romantic interests. A person with "a cast-iron ego" who spent a lifetime seeking
solace in God. Fiercely loyal to longtime friends, like
army buddy John Keenan, but likely to abandon others,
such as mentor Whit Burnett.

Nor can Salinger's legacy be fully assessed until his
unpublished fiction is released. When Salinger created
the J. D. Salinger Literary Trust, he was the sole trustee.
The Trust was assigned the copyright to all of Salinger's

work, with the express proviso that *The Catcher in the Rye* never be turned into a film.[272] More importantly, Salinger authorized the posthumous release of his unseen work produced over the last forty-five years of his life. When he died, his wife, Colleen Salinger, and his son, Matt, became co-executors of the Trust.

Because Salinger was writing for nearly fifty years without publishing, he left behind a lot of material. There are pages typed on his Underwood or Royal typewriters. And there are what Matt calls "squibs or fragments" on ordinary paper cut into eighths, "a lot of handwritten very small notes."[273] Creating digital files from Salinger's handwritten manuscripts and notes is difficult, so he has often had to type the words himself. He told the *Guardian* in 2019 that he expects to release some of the material in the next three to five years, which now suggests 2024 or 2025.

Still, much can be said about Salinger's legacy based on what we already know. To begin with, for all the hours he spent writing, J. D. Salinger published just four books: One legendary novel, *The Catcher in the Rye*, still a fixture on high school and college reading lists. One collection of nine short stories. And two volumes about the Glass siblings, each containing two stories. Only *Catcher* was an original book. The other three books were collections of previously published stories, nearly all of them reprinted from *The New Yorker*.

His remaining published stories, twenty-two in all, were printed in various other magazines, mainly from

1940 to 1948, but they were never anthologized in volumes of their own. Salinger also left behind seven unpublished stories, most of them available at the Firestone Library at Princeton University. Salinger regarded these early stories as part of his apprenticeship as a writer, best forgotten by future generations. (See appendix for a complete list of Salinger's fiction.)

Salinger did write another twenty-five or so stories, but they were never published and went missing decades ago. Most of them were written during World War II, that pre-Xerox era when copies were scarce. The lost stories, another casualty of war, are also a lost opportunity to assess Salinger's early work and judge his literary path to greatness.

In assessing his legacy, I think that Salinger's last-published fiction did not measure up to *The Catcher in the Rye*, *Nine Stories*, or even "Franny," a short, early Glass story. In this regard, he's no different from many other major writers of his era—for example, Saul Bellow, John Updike, Norman Mailer, or Bernard Malamud, whose published work declined in quality over their writing lifetimes. (One major exception: Philip Roth, whose later books were among his best.) While all of Salinger's books landed on the *New York Times* bestseller list,[274] his last three major stories were generally panned by reviewers. And from today's perspective, I think that "Zooey", "Seymour: An Introduction," and "Hapworth 16, 1924" do seem lesser works—far below Salinger's best.

Overall, Salinger was not a sociological writer dealing with the macro condition of life, but rather with the
micro world of an individual's inner life. "The Glass
stories tell us far more about the darkness of love and
self-hate than about the conditions of an urban Jewish
family in mid-century America," wrote literary critic
Ihab Hassan in 1957.[275]
Salinger was able to explore his characters' inner
life because his fiction, though sometimes thin on plot,
is especially strong on character and voice. His narra-
tives are sustained by his great gift for colloquial dialogue that captures the quotidian detail of time, place,
and mood. And like the early modernists, such as
James Joyce and Virginia Woolf, he created a stream
of consciousness that is psychologically revealing. *The
Catcher in the Rye* is Holden's sustained monologue,
rather Joycean without the sex.

In painting his scenes and creating his characters,
Salinger paid much attention to detail. Alfred Kazin, a
revered critic, was much amused: "Someday," he wrote,
"there will be a learned thesis on 'The Use of the Ash
Tray in J. D. Salinger's Stories:'"

> "No other writer has made so much of
> Americans lighting up, reaching for the
> ash tray, setting up the ash tray with one
> hand while reaching with the other hand
> for a ringing telephone."[276]

His weaknesses are evident, too. He sometimes had a tendency, as Updike put it in reviewing *Franny and Zooey*, toward "vehement editorializing." Updike especially disliked what he saw as Salinger's religious proselytizing. Others, echoing Updike, also attributed the decline in Salinger's fiction to his embrace of religious mysticism. Critic Ben Yagoda, who wrote a history of *The New Yorker*, called Salinger's later work a direction "that would eventually terminate in a dead end."[277]

Similarly, in a review of "Seymour: An Introduction," Granville Hicks quotes Buddy Glass trying to explain Seymour's behavior: "What was he, anyway? A saint? Thankfully, it isn't my responsibility to answer that one."[278] But Salinger does have an answer: he is clearly trying to make Seymour a contemporary saint.

Sometimes, I think Salinger was tendentious in choosing his targets. As a college dropout who never made it through his freshman year at two schools, he showed in both *The Catcher in the Rye* and *Franny and Zooey* his great disdain for academics, those "phony" intellectuals. Throughout his writing life, he also sneered at editors, who might change a word of the prose he labored over. And he loathed publishers, those profit-seeking dilettantes who vulgarized books by sensationalizing their covers and who dared to send review copies to book critics, a standard practice.

Salinger also idealized children. The young people in a Salinger story are usually precocious kids, projecting an extraordinary wisdom beyond their years.

Sometimes, they are deftly drawn: think of Phoebe or Esmé. But sometimes, they are human parables rather than realistic characters—none more so than Teddy, the boy genius, or Seymour, who lived on in the idolized memory of his siblings.

Some critics attributed the decline in Salinger's later fiction to his withdrawal from society. Salinger himself had speculated, on the dust jacket of *Franny and Zooey*, that he might one day "bog down, perhaps disappear entirely, in my own methods, locutions and mannerisms." Michiko Kakutani cited Salinger's own words in her review of "Hapworth 16, 1924," Salinger's last published story, when it was falsely rumored to be published as a book in 1997, some thirty-two years after it first appeared in *The New Yorker*. Writing in the *New York Times*, she said:

> "The falling off in his work...is a palpable consequence of Mr. Salinger's own Glass-like withdrawal from the public world: withdrawal feeding self-absorption and self-absorption feeding tetchy disdain."[279]

But Salinger needed to isolate, both to write and to meditate. The isolation was tolerable because of his religious belief in Vedanta, which stipulated that he withdraw to become closer to God. In effect, his writing became a spiritual act.

Rumor has it that there are many more Glass stories awaiting release, especially about Seymour, the sainted sibling, and his quest for God. Salinger's later writing is unlikely to revisit the Judaism of his youth or the other religions, such as Zen Buddhism, that he practiced before settling on Vedanta. I'd guess the later stories are infused with even more Vedanta religious teachings. Salinger is also said to have written a primer on Vedanta, similar in form to *The Gospel of Sri Ramakrishna*, which was Salinger's bible. In his will, Salinger donated a substantial amount of money to the Ramakrishna-Vivikenanda Center of New York, according to David Shields and Shane Salerno, who produced a PBS documentary on Salinger in 2013.[280]

Perhaps during his decades of literary isolation in Cornish, New Hampshire, Salinger did write some wonderful fiction—about the Glass family or otherwise. We'll soon find out. From the evidence at hand, more than fourteen years after his death, it seems improbable. I fear J. D. Salinger lost his literary way on his lonely road to religious epiphany.

••• END •••

APPENDIX

SALINGER'S PUBLISHED FICTION

1940:

"The Young Folks," *Story* magazine, March–April 1940.

"Go See Eddie," *University of Kansas City Review*, December 1940.

1941:

"The Hang of It," *Collier's*, July 12, 1941.

"The Heart of a Broken Story," *Esquire*, September 1941.

1942:

"The Long Debut of Lois Taggett," *Story* magazine, September–October 1942.

"Personal Notes on an Infantryman," *Collier's*, December 12, 1942.

1943:

"The Varioni Brothers," *Saturday Evening Post*, July 17, 1943.

1944:

"Both Parties Concerned," *Saturday Evening Post*, February 26, 1944.

"Soft-Boiled Sergeant," *Saturday Evening Post*, April 15, 1944.

"Last Day of the Last Furlough," *Saturday Evening Post*, July 15, 1944.

"Once a Week Won't Kill You," *Story* magazine, November–December 1944.

1945:

"Elaine," *Story* magazine, March–April 1945.

"A Boy in France," *Saturday Evening Post*, March 31, 1945

"This Sandwich Has No Mayonnaise," *Esquire*, October 1945.

"The Stranger," *Collier's*, December 1, 1945.

"I'm Crazy," *Collier's*, December 22, 1945. Adapted into *The Catcher in the Rye*.

1946:

"Slight Rebellion off Madison," *The New Yorker*, December 21, 1946. Adapted into *The Catcher in the Rye*.

1947:

"A Young Girl in 1941 with No Waist at All," *Mademoiselle*, May 1947.

"The Inverted Forest," *Cosmopolitan*, December 1947.

1948:

"A Perfect Day for Bananafish," *The New Yorker*, January 31, 1948.

"A Girl I Knew," *Good Housekeeping*, February 1948.

"Uncle Wiggily in Connecticut," *The New Yorker*, March 20, 1948.

"Just Before the War with the Eskimos," *The New Yorker*, June 5, 1948.

"Blue Melody," *Cosmopolitan*, September 1948.

1949:

"The Laughing Man," *The New Yorker*, March 19, 1949.

"Down at the Dinghy," *Harper's*, April 1949.

1950:

"For Esmé—With Love and Squalor," *The New Yorker*, April 8, 1950.

1951:

"Pretty Mouth and Green My Eyes," *The New Yorker*, July 14, 1951.

The Catcher in the Rye, Little, Brown, Boston, July 16, 1951. (First book.)

1952:

"De Daumier-Smith's Blue Period," *World Review*, May 1952.

1953:

"Teddy," *The New Yorker*, January 31, 1953.

Nine Stories, Little, Brown, Boston, April 6, 1953. (Second book.)

1955:

"Franny," *The New Yorker*, January 29, 1955.

"Raise High the Roofbeam, Carpenters," *The New Yorker*, November 19, 1955.

1957:

"Zooey," *The New Yorker*, May 4, 1957.

1959:

"Seymour: An Introduction," *The New Yorker*, June 6, 1959.

1961:

Franny and Zooey, Little, Brown, Boston, September 14, 1961. (Third book.)

1963:

Raise High the Roofbeam, Carpenters and Seymour: An Introduction. Little, Brown, Boston, January 28, 1963. (Fourth book.)

1965:

"Hapworth 16, 1924," *The New Yorker*, June 19, 1965.

SOURCES:

J. D. Salinger, An Annotated Bibliography, 1938–1981. By Jack R. Sublette, Garland Publishing, Inc., 1984.

Salinger. By David Shields and Shane Salerno, Simon & Schuster, 2013

SALINGER'S UNPUBLISHED MANUSCRIPTS

1941:

"Mrs. Hincher," sometimes called "Paula." (Harry Ransom Center, University of Texas).

1942:

"The Last and Best of the Peter Pans," (Firestone Library, Princeton University).

1944:

"The Children's Echelon," (Firestone Library, Princeton).

"Two Lonely Men," (Firestone Library, Princeton).

"The Magic Foxhole," (Firestone Library, Princeton).

1945:

"The Ocean Full of Bowling Balls," (Firestone Library, Princeton).

1946:

"Birthday Boy," (Harry Ransom Center, University of Texas).

SOURCE:
Deadcaulfields.com

SALINGER'S LOST MANUSCRIPTS

About twenty-five unpublished stories that Salinger is known to have written are missing. Their manuscripts have not been found, including some that were read by editors at *The New Yorker* but rejected for publication. Their loss makes it impossible to chart Salinger's progress as a writer in his early days.

Here is a list of some of these missing stories that scholars have identified:

1941:
    "The Fisherman" *
    "Lunch for Three" *
    "Monologue for a Watery Highball" *
    "I Went to School with Adolph Hitler" *

1942:
    "The Kissless Life of Reilly" *

    "Holden on the Bus" *

    "Men without Hemingway" *

1943:
    "The Broken Children"
    "Rex Passard on the Planet Mars"
    "Bitsy"
    "What Got into Curtis in the Woodshed" * *

1944:

"A Young Man in a Stuffed Shirt" **

1945:

"The Daughter of the Late Great Man" **

1948:

"The Boy in the People Shooting Hat" ***

1950:

"Requiem for the Phantom of the Opera" **

*Rejected by *The New Yorker*.

** Rejected by *Story* magazine.

***Rejected by *The New Yorker*, but partially incorporated into *The Catcher in the Rye*.

SOURCE:

Deadcaulfields.com

SELECTED BIBLIOGRAPHY
(IN CHRONOLOGICAL ORDER)

Henry Anatole Grunwald, editor: *Salinger: A Critical and Personal Portrait*. Harper and Brothers, New York, 1962.

Warren French: *J. D. Salinger*, Twayne Publishers, 1963. Revised edition: Bobbs-Merrill Educational Publishing, Indianapolis, 1976.

Jack R. Sublette: *J. D. Salinger: An Annotated Bibliography, 1938–1981*. Garland Publishing, Inc., 1984.

Ian Hamilton: *In Search of J. D. Salinger*. Random House, New York, 1988.

Thomas Kunkel: *Genius in Disguise: Harold Ross of The New Yorker*, Random House, New York, 1995.

Joyce Maynard: *At Home in the World, a Memoir*. Picador USA, New York, 1998.

Paul Alexander: *Salinger: A Biography.* Renaissance Books, Los Angeles, 1999.

Ben Yagoda: *The New Yorker and the World It Made.* Scribner, New York, 2000.

Margaret Salinger: *Dream Catcher: A Memoir.* Washington Square Press, New York, 2000.

Harold Bloom, editor: *Bloom's BioCritiques: J. D. Salinger.* Chelsea House Publishers, Philadelphia, 2002.

Eberhard Alsen: *A Reader's Guide to J. D. Salinger.* Greenwood Press, Westport, Connecticut, 2002

Kenneth Slawenski: *J. D. Salinger: A Life.* Random House, New York, 2010.

David Shields and Shane Salerno: *Salinger.* Simon & Schuster, New York, 2013.

Eberhard Alsen: *J. D. Salinger and the Nazis.* The University of Wisconsin Press, Madison, Wisconsin, 2018.

ENDNOTES

Introduction

1   Ron Charles, "J. D. Salinger at 100: Is The Catcher in the Rye Still Relevant?" *The Washington Post*, December 30, 2018. Also: www.goodreads.com/blog/show/1017-10-interesting-facts-about-the-catcher-in-the-rye. In 2019, Salinger's son, Matt Salinger, estimated *Catcher's* total sales at 72 million copies. (See "Matt Salinger Wants to Put the Record Straight," by Erica Wagner. Penguin Books, London, June 11, 2019.)

2   Lidija Haas, "Matt Salinger: 'My Father was Writing for 50 Years Without Publishing. That's a Lot of Material.'" *The Guardian*, February 1, 2019. Also, David Shields and Shane Salerno, *Salinger*, Simon & Schuster, New York, 2013.

3   In Vedanta teachings, sex in marriage is allowed, but only for the purpose of procreation.

4   J. D. Salinger, "A Young Girl in 1941 with No Waist at All," *Mademoiselle*, May 1947.

Chapter 1: "All That David Copperfield Kind of Crap"

5   Margaret Salinger, *Dream Catcher*, Washington Square Press, New York, 2000. P. 17.

6   Benjamin Ivry, "On J. D. Salinger's 100th Birthday, His Not-so secret Jewish History," An interview with biographer Kenneth Slawenski, *The Forward*, December 21, 2018.

7   Margaret Salinger, *Dream Catcher*, Washington Square Press, New York, 2000. P. 20.

8   Paul Alexander, *Salinger: A Biography*, Renaissance Books, Los Angeles, 1999. P. 33.

9   Margaret Salinger, *Dream Catcher*, Washington Square Press, New York, 2000. P. 33–34.

10   Paul Alexander, *Salinger: A Biography*, Renaissance Books, Los Angeles, 1999. P. 38

11   Margaret Salinger, *Dream Catcher*, Washington Square Press, New York, 2000. P. 33.

12   Ibid. P. 24.

13   Kenneth Slawenski, *J. D. Salinger: A Life*, Random House, New York, 2010. P. 19.

14   Warren French, *J. D. Salinger*, Bobbs-Merrill Educational Publish, Indianapolis, 1976. P. 23

15   Paul Alexander, *Salinger: A Biography*, Renaissance Books, Los Angeles, 1999. P. 54.

16   Molly Schwartzburg: "J. D. Salinger at the Harry Ransom Center," *Ransom Center Magazine*, Austin, Texas, February 25, 2020.

17   Sarah Norris, "How [Elizabeth Murray] Befriended—and Betrayed—J. D. Salinger," *Chapter 16*, Nashville, Tennessee, December 8, 2011.

18   *New York Times*, "FTC Bans Price Fixing by Cheese Companies," October 5, 1940; "15 Named in Fixing of Cheese Prices," July 2, 1941; and September 7, 1944. See also David Shields and Shane Salerno, *Salinger*, Simon & Schuster, New York, 2013. P. 33.

19   Eberhard Alsen, *Salinger and the Nazis*, University of Wisconsin Press, Madison, 2018. P. 17.

20   Ibid. P. 18.

21   Kenneth Slawenski, *J. D. Salinger: A Life*, Random House, New York, 2010. P. 164.

22   Charles McGrath, "J. D. Salinger, Literary Recluse, Dies at 91," *New York Times*, January 28, 2010.

23   Ian Hamilton, *In Search of J. D. Salinger*, Faber and Faber, London, 1988. P. 44–45.

24   Paul Alexander, *Salinger: A Biography*, Renaissance Books, Los Angeles, 1999. P. 52–53.
25   J. D. Salinger, "Musings of a Social Soph: The Skipped Diploma," *Ursinus Weekly*, October 10, 1938. See also: Kenneth Slawenski, *J. D. Salinger: A Life,* Random House, New York, 2010. P. 24.
26   Kenneth Slawenski, *J. D. Salinger: A Life,* Random House, New York, 2010. P. 27.

Chapter 2: The Mentor on Morningside Heights
27   Paul Hond, "The Teacher Who Inspired J. D. Salinger and a Generation of American Writers," *Columbia Magazine*, New York, Winter 2018–19. Originally entitled "Upper West Side Stories."
28   Ibid.
29   Jerome Salinger, "The Young Folks," *Story* Magazine, March–April 1940.
30   Ibid.
31   Ian Hamilton, *J. D. Salinger: A Writing Life*. Random House, New York, 1986, bound galleys. P. 46.
32   Kenneth Slawenski, *J. D. Salinger: A Life,* Random House, New York, 2010. P. 38, 41.
33   Warren French, *J. D. Salinger*, Bobbs-Merrill Educational Publish, Indianapolis, 1976. P. 25.
34   Paul Hond, "The Teacher Who Inspired J. D. Salinger and a Generation of American Writers," *Columbia Magazine*, New York, Winter 2018–19.
35   Ibid.
36   J. D. Salinger, "A Salute to Whit Burnett (1899–1972)," *Fiction Writer's Handbook*, by Hallie & Whit Burnett, Harper & Row, New York, 1975. P. 187–188.

Chapter 3: Salinger at War
37   Ian Hamilton, *J. D. Salinger: A Writing Life*. Random House, New York, 1986, bound galleys. P. 53. Also: Kenneth

Slawenski, *J. D. Salinger: A Life,* Random House, New York, 2010. P. 43.

38 David Shields and Shane Salerno, *Salinger,* Simon & Schuster, New York, 2013. P. 69.

39 The three stories in *The Saturday Evening Post* were: "Both Parties Concerned," (February 26, 1944); "Soft-Boiled Sergeant," (April 15, 1944); and "Last Day of the Last Furlough," (July 15, 1944).

40 Margaret Salinger, *Dream Catcher,* Washington Square Press, New York, 2000. P. 53.

41 Kenneth Slawenski, *J. D. Salinger: A Life,* Random House, New York, 2010. P. 106–107.

42 Ibid. P. 96.

43 Salinger letter to Whit Burnett, June 28, 1944. Quoted in Eberhard Alsen, *Salinger and the Nazis,* University of Wisconsin Press, Madison, 2018. P. 53.

44 Salinger letter to Whit Burnett, September 9, 1944. Quoted in Eberhard Alsen, *Salinger and the Nazis,* University of Wisconsin Press, Madison, 2018. P. 64.

45 Ian Hamilton, *In Search of J. D. Salinger,* Faber and Faber, London, 1988. P. 85–86. Also, Kenneth Slawenski, *J. D. Salinger: A Life,* Random House, New York, 2010. P. 100–101.

46 John Skow, "Sonny, an Introduction," *Time* magazine, September 15, 1961.

47 Kenneth Slawenski, *J. D. Salinger: A Life,* Random House, New York, 2010. P. 139.

48 John Keenan letter to Matt Salinger after J. D. Salinger's death in January 2010. The letter was displayed at the Salinger exhibition at the New York Public Library in 2019. It was discussed in a subsequent article, posted on *The Daily Beast* by Nicolaus Mills, entitled, "Son of Sam Cop Pays Tribute to Army Buddy Sgt. J. D. Salinger."

49 David Shields and Shane Salerno, *Salinger,* Simon & Schuster, New York, 2013. P. 105.

50   Ibid. P. 107.

51   Ibid. P. 125, 138.

52   Ibid. P. 147.

53   Kenneth Slawenski, *J. D. Salinger: A Life,* Random House, New York, 2010. P. 122.

54   Margaret Salinger, *Dream Catcher*, Washington Square Press, New York, 2000. P. 43.

55   Barbara   Graustark,   "Newsmakers,"   *Newsweek,* July 17, 1978.

56   Margaret Salinger, *Dream Catcher*, Washington Square Press, New York, 2000. P. 44.

57   Ibid. P. 55.

58   Salinger letter to Ernest Hemingway, July 1945. Quoted in Eberhard Alsen, *Salinger and the Nazis*, University of Wisconsin Press, Madison, 2018. P. 89.

59   David Shields and Shane Salerno, *Salinger*, Simon & Schuster, New York, 2013. P. 167. Also: Eberhard Alsen, *Salinger and the Nazis*, University of Wisconsin Press, Madison, 2018. P. 82-93.

60   Salinger letter to Elizabeth Murray, May 13, 1945. Quoted in Eberhard Alsen, *Salinger and the Nazis*, University of Wisconsin Press, Madison, 2018. P. 92.

61   Salinger letter to Ernest Hemingway, July 1945. Quoted in Eberhard Alsen, *Salinger and the Nazis*, University of Wisconsin Press, Madison, 2018. P. 89.

62   Charles Poore, *The New York Times,* April 9, 1953.

63   Margaret Salinger, *Dream Catcher*, Washington Square Press, New York, 2000. P. 68

64   J. D. Salinger, "Backstage with Esquire," *Esquire,* October 1945

Chapter 4: The German Connection

65   Eberhard Alsen, *Salinger and the Nazis*, Univ of Wisconsin Press, Madison, 2018. P.92.

66   Ibid. P. 66–67.

67   Ibid. P. 39–44

68   Kenneth Slawenski, *J. D. Salinger: A Life,* Random House, New York, 2010. P. 113.

69   John Keenan letter to Matt Salinger after J. D. Salinger's death in January 2010. The letter was displayed at the Salinger exhibition at the New York Public Library in 2019.

70   Eberhard Alsen, *Salinger and the Nazis,* University of Wisconsin Press, Madison, 2018. P. 80–81.

Chapter 5: Jerry and His War Bride

71   Eberhard Alsen, *Salinger and the Nazis,* University of Wisconsin Press, Madison, 2018. P. 99–109.

72   Ian Hamilton, *In Search of J. D. Salinger,* Faber and Faber, London, 1988. P. 90, 97

73   Kenneth Slawenski, *J. D. Salinger: A Life,* Random House, New York, 2010. P. 145.

74   Eberhard Alsen, *Salinger and the Nazis,* University of Wisconsin Press, Madison, 2018. P.106.

75   Ibid. P. 66.

76   Thomas Beller, *J. D. Salinger: The Escape Artist,* Amazon Publishing, Seattle, 2014. P. 142. Also: Margaret Salinger, *Dream Catcher,* Washington Square Press, New York, 2000. P. 359.

77   Eberhard Alsen, *Salinger and the Nazis,* Univ. of Wisconsin Press, Madison, 2018. P. 102.

78   Ibid. P. 131.

Chapter 6: "Tall, Dark, and Handsome"

79   Kenneth Slawenski, *J. D. Salinger: A Life,* Random House, New York, 2010. P. 150.

80   Ian Hamilton, *In Search of J. D. Salinger,* Faber and Faber, London, 1988. David Shields and Shane Salerno, *Salinger,* Simon & Schuster, New York, 2013. P. 276.

81   Ian Hamilton, *In Search of J. D. Salinger,* Faber and Faber, London, 1988 P. 124

82   Ibid. P. 127.

83   David Shields and Shane Salerno, *Salinger*, Simon & Schuster, New York, 2013. P. 190.

84   A. E. Hotchner, *Choice People*, William Morrow, New York, 1984. P. 67.

85   Ibid. P. 65.

86   David Shields and Shane Salerno, *Salinger*, Simon & Schuster, New York, 2013 P. 194.

87   Ibid. P. 213, 215–216.

88   I later became friends with Himan Brown when he served on the board of CUNY TV. He donated money for scholarships to the CUNY Graduate School of Journalism when I was the Dean.

89   Kenneth Slawenski, *J. D. Salinger: A Life,* Random House, New York, 2010. P. 217.

Chapter 7: Here at *The New Yorker*

90   Ben Yagoda, *About Town: The New Yorker and the World It Made*, Scribner, New York, 2000. P.233.

91   Paul Alexander, *Salinger: A Biography*, Renaissance Books, Los Angeles, 1999. P. 90.

92   Ibid. P.90.

93   Ibid. P. 93.

94   Ben Yagoda, *About Town: The New Yorker and the World It Made*, Scribner, New York, 2000. P. 234.

95   Ibid. P. 234.

96   Margaret Salinger, *Dream Catcher*, Washington Square Press, New York, 2000. P. 19.

97   Paul Alexander, *Salinger: A Biography*, Renaissance Books, Los Angeles, 1999. P. 125.

98   Warren French, *J. D. Salinger*, Bobbs-Merrill Educational Publish, Indianapolis, 1976. P. 80–84.

99   Kenneth Slawenski, *J. D. Salinger: A Life,* Random House, New York, 2010. P. 166–167.

100   Ibid. P. 166–167.

101   Ibid. P.167.

102   Kenneth Slawenski, *J. D. Salinger: A Life,* Random House, New York, 2010. P. 187

103   Dan Wakefield, "Salinger and the Search for Love," *New World Writing #14, 1958.* Reprinted in *Salinger: A Critical and Personal Portrait,* edited by Henry Anatole Grunwald, Harper & Brothers, New York, 1962. P. 181–183.

104   Paul Alexander, *Salinger: A Biography*, Renaissance Books, Los Angeles, 1999. P. 147.

105   Ibid. P. 148.

106   S. N. Behrman, "The Vision of the Innocent," *The New Yorker*, August 4, 1951.

107   Ben Yagoda, *About Town: The New Yorker and the World It Made*, Scribner, New York, 2000. P. 240.

108   Thomas Kunkel, *Genius in Disguise: Harold Ross of The New Yorker*, Random House, New York, 1995. Page 249.

109   Kenneth Slawenski, *J. D. Salinger: A Life,* Random House, New York, 2010. P. 220.

110   Paul Alexander, *Salinger: A Biography*, Renaissance Books, Los Angeles, 1999. P. 159.

111   Kenneth Slawenski, *J. D. Salinger: A Life,* Random House, New York, 2010. P. 228.

112   Scott Elledge, *E.B. White: A Biography*, Norton, New York, 1984. P. 317.

113   Kenneth Slawenski, *J. D. Salinger: A Life,* Random House, New York, 2010. P. 228-229.

114   Paul Alexander and Ben Yagoda quoted in *Salinger* by David Shields and Shane Salerno, Simon & Schuster, New York, 2013. P. 340–341.

115   Kenneth Slawenski, *J. D. Salinger: A Life,* Random House, New York, 2010. P. 229. Also: Thomas Beller, *J. D. Salinger: The Escape Artist*, Amazon Publishing, Seattle, 2014. P. 170.

116   Kenneth Slawenski, *J. D. Salinger: A Life,* Random House, New York, 2010. P. 286.

117   Ibid. P. 287.

118   Michiko Kakutani. "From Salinger, a New Dash of Mystery," *The New York Times*, February 20, 1997.

Chapter 8: Holden in the Rye

119   Ian Hamilton, *In Search of J. D. Salinger,* Faber and Faber, London, 1988. P. 117.

120   Paul Alexander, *Salinger: A Biography*, Renaissance Books, Los Angeles, 1999. P. 93.

121   "Back Stage with Esquire," *Esquire,* October 24, 1945. P. 34.

122   Giroux's account appears in Ian Hamilton, *In Search of J. D. Salinger,* Faber and Faber, London, 1988. P. 109, and in Paul Alexander, *Salinger: A Biography*, Renaissance Books, Los Angeles, 1999. P. 135–136.

123   Kenneth Slawenski, *J. D. Salinger: A Life,* Random House, New York, 2010. P. 197. Also: Thomas Beller, *J. D. Salinger: The Escape Artist*, Amazon Publishing, Seattle, 2014. P. 178.

124   Ian Hamilton, *In Search of J. D. Salinger,* Faber and Faber, London, 1988. P. 115.

125   Paul Alexander, *Salinger: A Biography*, Renaissance Books, Los Angeles, 1999. P. 151.

126   Ian Hamilton, *J.D. Salinger: A Writing Life,* Random House, New York, 1986. Bound galley, P.111.

127   James Stern, "Aw, the World's a Crumby Place," *New York Times Book Review*, July 15, 1951.

128   Nash K. Burger, "Books of the Times," *The New York Times,* July 16, 1951.

129   New York Herald Tribune Book Review, August 19, 1951. P. 2.

130   Paul Levine, "The Development of the Misfit Hero," *Twentieth Century Literature*, 1958.

131   Harold Bloom, *J. D. Salinger*, Bloom's BioCritiques, Broomall, PA, 2002. P. 2.

132   S. N. Behrman, "The Vision of the Innocent," *The New Yorker*, August 4, 1951.

133   Ian Hamilton, *In Search of J. D. Salinger*, Faber and Faber, London, 1988. P. 155.

134   Warren French, *J. D. Salinger*, Bobbs-Merrill Educational Publishing, Indianapolis, 1976. P. 162.

135   John Skow, "Sonny, an Introduction," *Time* magazine, September 15, 1961.

136   Louis Menand, "Holden at Fifty: *The Catcher in the Rye* and What it Spawned," *The New Yorker*, October 1, 2001.

137   Dana Czapnik, "From Everyteen to Annoying: Are Today's Readers Turning on *The Catcher in the Rye?*" *The Guardian*, August 1, 2019.

138   Alfred Kazin, "J. D. Salinger: Everybody's Favorite," *The Atlantic*, August 1961.

139   Dana Czapnik, "From Everyteen to Annoying: Are Today's Readers Turning on *The Catcher in the Rye?*" *The Guardian*, August 1, 2019.

140   Ron Charles, "J. D. Salinger at 100: Is The Catcher in the Rye Still Relevant?" *The Washington Post*, December 30, 2018. Also: www.goodreads.com/blog/show/1017-10-interesting-facts-about-the-catcher-in-the-rye.

Chapter 9: From Seymour to Teddy

141   The nine stories are: "A Perfect Day for Bananafish," "Uncle Wiggily in Connecticut," "Just Before the War with the Eskimos," "The Laughing Man," "Down at the Dinghy," "For Esmé—with Love and Squalor," "Pretty Mouth and Green My Eyes," "De Daumier-Smith's Blue Period," and "Teddy."

142   Frederick L. Glynn and Joseph L. Blotner, "One Hand Clapping," *The Fiction of J. D. Salinger*, University of Pittsburgh Press. Reprinted in *Salinger: A Critical and Personal Portrait*, edited by Henry Anatole Grunwald, 1962. Harper & Brothers, New York. P.109–113

143   Arthur Mizener, "The Love Story of J. D. Salinger," *Harper's*, February 1959.

144 Charles Poore, "Books of The Times," *The New York Times*, April 9, 1953.

145 Eudora Welty, "Threads of Innocence, *The New York Times Book Review,* April 5, 1953.

146 Gilbert Highet, "New Wine, Old Bottles." *Harper's,* December 1953.

147 Paul Alexander, *Salinger: A Biography*, Renaissance Books, Los Angeles, 1999. P. 200–202.

148 Kenneth Slawenski, *J. D. Salinger: A Life,* Random House, New York, 2010. P. 325.

149 Paul Alexander, *Salinger: A Biography*, Renaissance Books, Los Angeles, 1999. P. 174.

Chapter 10: Retreat to Cornish

150 Eloise Perry Hazard, "Eight Fiction Finds," *Saturday Review*, February 16, 1952. See also: Ian Hamilton, *In Search of J. D. Salinger,* Faber and Faber, London, 1988. P. 121–122.

151 New England Historical Society, Cornish, NH, Harlakenden House.

152 Margaret Salinger, *Dream Catcher*, Washington Square Press, New York, 2000.

153 Mel Elfin, *Newsweek*, May 30, 1960.

154 Salinger's relationship with the high school students has been mentioned in several early books: Warren French, *J.D. Salinger*, Bobbs Merrill Educational Publishing, Indianapolis, 1976. P. 66; Ian Hamilton, *In Search of J. D. Salinger,* Faber and Faber, London, 1988. P. 137-139; and Paul Alexander, *Salinger: A Biography*, Renaissance Books, Los Angeles, 1999. P. 177-178.

155 David Shields and Shane Salerno, *Salinger*, Simon & Schuster, New York, 2013. P. 331.

156 Ian Hamilton, *In Search of J. D. Salinger,* Faber and Faber, London, 1988. P. 153–154.

157 David Shields and Shane Salerno, *Salinger*, Simon & Schuster, New York, 2013. P. 320. Kenneth Slawenski, J.D. Salinger: A Writing Life, Random House, New York, 2010. P. 219.

158 Margaret Salinger, *Dream Catcher*, Washington Square Press, New York, 2000. P. 5–6.

159 Ibid.

160 Kenneth Slawenski, *J. D. Salinger: A Life*, Random House, New York, 2010. P. 251.

161 David Shields and Shane Salerno, *Salinger*, Simon & Schuster, New York, 2013. P. 324.

162 Paul Alexander, *Salinger: A Biography*, Renaissance Books, Los Angeles, 1999. P. 186.

163 Phoebe Hoban, "The Salinger File," *New York* Magazine, June 15, 1987.

164 David Shields and Shane Salerno, *Salinger*, Simon & Schuster, New York, 2013. P. 329.

165 Paul Alexander, *Salinger: A Biography*, Renaissance Books, Los Angeles, 1999. P. 188.

166 Margaret Salinger, *Dream Catcher*, Washington Square Press, New York, 2000. P. 185–187.

167 J. D. Salinger, "A Young Girl in 1941 with No Waist at All," *Mademoiselle*, May 1947.

168 Paul Alexander, *Salinger: a Biography*, Renaissance Books, Los Angeles, 1999. P. 236–237.

169 Source: Radcliffe College. See Paul Alexander, *Salinger: A Biography*, Renaissance Books, Los Angeles, 1999. P. 291.

170 Ibid. P. 290.

171 Ian Hamilton, *In Search of J. D. Salinger*, Faber and Faber, London, 1988. P. 190.

172 Paul Alexander, *Salinger: A Biography*, Renaissance Books, Los Angeles, 1999. P. 293–294.

Chapter 11: Religious Zeal

173 Both Glass parents were former vaudeville performers, known professionally as Gallagher and Glass on the touring circuit.

174 Ihab Hassan, "The Rare Quixotic Gesture," Reprinted in *Salinger: A Critical and Personal Portrait*, edited by

Henry Anatole Grunwald, Harper & Brothers, New York, 1962. P. 147.

175   Warren French, *J.D. Salinger*, Bobbs-Merrill Educational Publishing, 1976. P. 139. Also, Kenneth Slawenski, *J. D. Salinger: A Life*, Random House, New York, 2010. P. 262.

176   Warren French, *J. D. Salinger*, Bobbs-Merrill Educational Publishing, 1976. P. 142.

177   John Skow, "Sonny, an Introduction," *Time* magazine, September 15, 1961.

178   Alfred Kazin (*The Atlantic*, August 1961); Joan Didion (*National Review*, November 18, 1961); Mary McCarthy (*Observer Weekend Review*, June 3, 1962); and Maxwell Geismar (*Salinger: A Critical and Personal Portrait*, edited by Henry Grunwald, 1962.)

179   Warren French, *J. D. Salinger*, Bobbs-Merrill Educational Publishing, 1976. P. 148.

180   Maxwell Geismar, "The Wise Child and *The New Yorker* School of Fiction,' in *Salinger: a Critical and Personal Portrait*, edited by Henry Anatole Grunwald, Harper and Brothers, New York, 1962. P.105.

181   John Updike, "Anxious Days for the Glass Family," *The New York Times Book Review*, September 17, 1961.

182   Janet Malcolm, "Justice to J. D. Salinger," *The New York Review of Books*, June 21, 2001.

183   Louis Menand, "*The Catcher in the Rye* and What it Spawned," *The New Yorker*, October 1, 2001.

184   Norman Mailer, "Evaluations: Quick and Expansive Comments on the Talent in the Room," *Advertisements for Myself*, G. P. Putnam's Sons, New York, 1959. P. 467.

185   John Updike, "Anxious Days for the Glass Family," *The New York Times Book Review*, September 17, 1961.

186   Orville Prescott, "Books of the Times," *The New York Times*, January 28, 1963.

187   Ibid.

188   Irving Howe, *New York Times Book Review*, April 7, 1963.

189 Warren French, *J. D. Salinger*, Bobbs-Merrill Educational Publishing, Indianapolis. 1976. P. 155.

190 Kenneth Slawenski, *J. D. Salinger: A Life*, Random House, New York, 2010. P. 306.

191 Margaret Salinger, *Dream Catcher*, Washington Square Press, New York, 2000. Introduction, P. xi.

Chapter 12: "To See God"

192 A. L. Bardach, "What Did J. D. Salinger, Leo Tolstoy, and Sarah Bernhardt Have in Common?" *The Wall Street Journal*, March 30, 2012.

193 Ramakrishna-Vivekenanda Center, New York.

194 A. L. Bardach, "What Did J. D. Salinger, Leo Tolstoy, and Sarah Bernhardt Have in Common?" *The Wall Street Journal*, March 30, 2012.

195 Ibid.

196 Morgan Library & Museum, Press Release, April 3, 2013.

197 www.learnreligions.com

198 Margaret Salinger, *Dream Catcher*, Washington Square Press, New York, 2000. P. 91.

199 A. L. Bardach, "What Did J. D. Salinger, Leo Tolstoy, and Sarah Bernhardt Have in Common?" *The Wall Street Journal*, March 30, 2012.

200 Dipti Pattanaik, "The Holy Refusal: A Vedantic Interpretation of J. D. Salinger's Silence," *Melus*, Vol. 23, No. 2, Oxford University Press, Summer, 1998.

201 John Updike, "Anxious Days for the Glass Family," *The New York Times Book Review*, September 17, 1961."

Chapter 13: "The Last Minutes of Her Girlhood"

202 Salinger had written a letter to *Harper's* magazine earlier in 1949 complaining about contributors' notes. He mentioned that "I almost always write about very young people." *Harper's* went ahead and crafted its own contributors' note from his letter to accompany his story "Down at the

Dinghy," which ran in the April 1949 issue. The magazine paraphrased Salinger this way: "His present story is characteristic in that it is about very young people." See Paul Alexander, *Salinger: A Biography*, Renaissance Books, Los Angeles, 1999. P. 131–132.

203 Henry Grunwald, *Salinger: A Critical and Personal Portrait*, Harper & Brothers, New York, 1962. Introduction, P. xvii.

204 Adam Kirsch, "Did Salinger Go Awry?" www.tabletmag. com. January 2, 2019.

205 J. D. Salinger, "A Young Girl in 1941 with No Waist at All," *Mademoiselle*, May 1947.

206 Paul Alexander, *Salinger: A Biography*, Renaissance Books, Los Angeles, 1999. P. 70–72.

207 David Shields and Shane Salerno, *Salinger*, Simon & Schuster, New York, 2013. P. 91–92

208 Ibid. P. 91–93.

209 Paul Alexander, *Salinger: A Biography*, Renaissance Books, Los Angeles. 1999. P. 84–87. Also, Arnold H. Lubasch, "A Salinger Biography is Blocked," *The New York Times*, January 30, 1987.

210 The story of Salinger's relationship with Jean Miller is told in: David Shields and Shane Salerno, *Salinger*, Simon & Schuster, New York, 2013. P. 200–242.

211 Salinger documentary, *American Masters*, PBS, January 21, 2013. David Shields and Shane Salerno.

212 David Shields and Shane Salerno, *Salinger*, Simon & Schuster, New York, 2013. P.241

213 Ibid. P. 234.

214 Ibid. P. 239.

215 Ibid. Page 220.

216 Joyce Maynard, *At Home in the World*, Picador, New York, 1998. P. 89.

217 Ibid. P.80.

218 Ibid. P. 88.

219 Margaret Salinger, *Dream Catcher*, Washington Square Press, New York, 2000. P. 360.

220 Joyce Maynard, *At Home in the World*, Picador, New York, 1998. P. 149.

221 Ibid. P. 206–207.

222 Kenneth Slawenski, *J. D. Salinger: A Life,* Random House, New York, 2010. P. 397.

223 Maureen Dowd, "Leech Women in Love!" *The New York Times*, Op-Ed page, May 19, 1999.

224 Joyce Carol Oates, "Words of Love, Priced to Sell," *The New York Times,* May 18, 1999.

225 Joyce Maynard, "Was She J. D. Salinger's Predator or His Prey," *The New York Times*, Op-Ed page, September 5, 2018.

226 Liz Gotthelf, "Famed Author's Letter Still Available," *Portland Press Herald*, September 30, 2015.

227 Paul Alexander, *Salinger: A Biography*, Renaissance Books, Los Angeles, 1999. P. 288.

228 For example, see "An Unlikely J. D. Salinger Hollywood Tale," by Marvin Kitman, *Newsday,* December 14, 1987.

229 Paul Alexander, *Salinger: A Biography*, Renaissance Books, Los Angeles, 1999. P. 273–274

230 Joyce Maynard, *At Home in the World*, Picador, New York, 1998. P. 326–331.

231 Ibid. P. 331.

Chapter 14: Sightings and Skirmishes

232 Margaret Salinger, *Dream Catcher*, Washington Square Press, New York, 2000. P.185–187.

233 David Shields and Shane Salerno, *Salinger*, Simon & Schuster, New York, 2013. P. 371–375.

234 Ian Hamilton, *J. D. Salinger: A Writing Life,* Random House, New York, bound galleys. P. 105.

235 Mel Elfin, "The Mysterious J. D. Salinger: His Woodsy Secluded life," *Newsweek,* May 30, 1960

236 John Skow, "Sonny, an Introduction," *Time* magazine, September 15, 1961.

237 Ernest Havemann, "The Search for the Mysterious J. D. Salinger," *Life* magazine, November 3, 1961.

238 For the record, both Mel Elfin and Ed Kosner were colleagues of mine at *Newsweek* years later in the 1970s. Elfin, who was the Washington bureau chief when I was the National Affairs editor, died on September 22, 2018. Ed Kosner, still a friend of mine, was the editor of *Newsweek* for most of my five years at the magazine.

239 Edward Kosner, "The Private World of J. D. Salinger," *New York Post Magazine*, April 30, 1961.

240 Paul Alexander, *Salinger: a Biography*, Renaissance Books, Los Angeles, 1999. P. 248–250

241 Lacey Fosburgh, "J. D. Salinger Speaks about His Silence," *The New York Times*, November 3, 1974.

242 Paul Alexander, *Salinger: A Biography*, Renaissance Books, Los Angeles, 1999. P. 259–263.

243 Betty Eppes, "What I Did Last Summer," The Paris Review, Summer 1981.

244 Brin-Jonathan Butler, "Woman with Only Recording of J. D. Salinger Will Take Tape to Grave," *Bloomberg Businessweek*, July 29, 2021.

245 Paul Alexander, *Salinger: A Biography*, Renaissance Books, Los Angeles, 1999 P. 288–289.

246 Ian Hamilton, *In Search of J. D. Salinger*, Faber and Faber, London, 1988. P. 190–212. Hamilton's book presents his first-person account of his legal battle with Salinger.

247 Phoebe Hoban, "The Salinger File," *New York* Magazine. June 15, 1987.

248 Paul Alexander, *Salinger: A Biography*, Renaissance Books, Los Angeles, 1999. P. 284.

249 Arnold H. Lubasch, "A Salinger Biography is Blocked," *The New York Times*, January 30, 1987.

250 Ian Hamilton, *In Search of J. D. Salinger*, Faber and Faber, London, 1988. P. 210.

Chapter 15: Father Figure

251 Margaret Salinger, *Dream Catcher*, Washington Square Press, New York, 2000. P. 96, 194. See also: Dinitia Smith, "Salinger's Daughter's Truths as Mesmerizing as His Fiction," *The New York Times,* August 30, 2000.

252 Margaret Salinger, *Dream Catcher*, Washington Square Press, New York, 2000. P. 115.

253 Lidija Haas, "Matt Salinger: 'My Father was Writing for 50 Years Without Publishing. That's a Lot of Material.'" *The Guardian*, February 1, 2019.

254 Janet Malcolm, "Justice to J. D. Salinger," *New York Review of Books*, June 21, 2001.

255 Dinitia Smith, "Salinger's Daughter's Truths as Mesmerizing as His Fiction," *The New York Times,* August 30, 2000.

256 Ibid.

257 Margaret Salinger, *Dream Catcher*, Washington Square Press, New York, 2000. P. 7.

258 Ibid. P.154.

259 Kenneth Slawenski, *J. D. Salinger: A Life,* Random House, New York, 2010. P. 375.

260 Lidija Haas, "Matt Salinger: 'My Father was Writing for 50 Years Without Publishing. That's a Lot of Material.'" *The Guardian*, February 1, 2019.

261 Margaret Salinger, *Dream Catcher*, Washington Square Press, New York, 2000. P. 364.

262 Ibid. P. 399

263 Ibid. P. 415.

264 Ibid. P. 415–417.

265 Ibid. P. 422.

266 Linton Weeks, "The Writer's Daughter," *Washington Post,* September 1, 2000.

267 Paul Corkery, "Solitude May be Bliss for Author J. D. Salinger, but to Son Matt, all the World's a Stage," *People* magazine, October 31, 1983.

268 Lidija Haas, "Matt Salinger: 'My Father was Writing for 50 Years Without Publishing. That's a Lot of Material.'" *The Guardian*, February 1, 2019.

269 Ibid.

270 Paul Corkery, "Solitude May be Bliss for Author J. D. Salinger, but to Son Matt, all the World's a Stage," *People* magazine, October 31, 1983.

Chapter 16: Salinger's Legacy

271 Charles McGrath, "J. D. Salinger, Literary Recluse, Dies at 91," *The New York Times*, January 29, 2010.

272 David Shields and Shane Salerno, *Salinger*, Simon & Schuster, New York, 2013. P. 574.

273 Lidija Haas, "Matt Salinger: 'My Father was Writing for 50 Years Without Publishing. That's a Lot of Material.'" *The Guardian*, February 1, 2019.

274 All four of Salinger's books made the New York Times best-seller list: *The Catcher in the Rye* reached number four, *Nine Stories* made it to ninth place, *Franny and Zooey* hit number one, as did *Raise High the Roof Beam, Carpenters and Seymour, an Introduction*.

275 Ihab Hassan, "The Rare Quixotic Gesture," Reprinted in *Salinger: A Critical and Personal Portrait*, edited by Henry Grunwald, Harper & Brothers, New York, 1962. P. 138–163.

276 Alfred Kazin, "J. D. Salinger, Everybody's Favorite," *The Atlantic*, August 1961.

277 Ben Yagoda, "About Town: *The New Yorker* and the World It Made," Scribner, New York, 2000. P. 285.

278 Granville Hicks, "The Search for Wisdom," *Saturday Review*, July 25, 1959.

279 Michiko Kakutani, "From Salinger, a New Dash of Mystery," *The New York Times*, February 20, 1997.

280 David Shields and Shane Salerno, *Salinger*, Simon & Schuster, New York, 2013. P. 575.

INDEX

A

Ace Books, 101
Adao, Paul, 164
Advaita Vedanta Hinduism, 133
Alabama, University of, 94
Alexander, Paul, 142, 149, 151
Algonquin Hotel, 76, 156
Alsen, Eberhard, 42, 50, 51-55
Altras, Jack, 38
"Am I Banging my Head Against the Wall?" 31, 64, 147
Andover, 175, 182
Anti-Semitism, 16, 118-119
Atlantic monthly, 87
At Home in the World, 149

B

Baton Rouge Advocate, 163
Battle of the Bulge, 40, 42
The Beautiful and Damned, 60
Becker, Betsy Jane, 182
Behrman, S.N., 73, 92

Bellow, Saul, 10, 11, 27, 126, 187
Blaney, Shirlie, 106
"Blue Melody," 59
"A Boy in France," 34, 48
"The Boy in the People Shooting Hat," 69
Book-of-the-Month Club, 86
Boston Edison, 176
Boston Symphony Orchestra, 177
Boston University, 176
Brandeis University, 176
Brearley School, 142
Brown, Andreas, 155, 160, 169
Brown, Himan, 60
Buchenwald, 20, 42
Buddhism: See Zen Buddhism
Burnett, Hallie, 27-29
Burnett, Whit, 22-30, 32, 33, 35, 36, 83, 84, 107, 141, 164, 165, 185

C

The Caine Mutiny, 83
Callagy, Robert, 169
Cameron, Angus, 86
Camp Wigwam, 15
Captain America, 182
Carroll, Lewis, 102
The Catcher in the Rye, 9, 13,
  15, 16, 21, 31, 33, 35, 38,
  47, 57, 60, 65, 69, 72, 73,
  75, 79, 83-88, 91-96, 100-
  101,103, 105, 106, 121,
  123-125,133, 137, 146,
  153, 157, 165, 175, 184,
  186-189
Caulfield, Holden, 10, 13, 16,
  31, 35, 37, 38, 47, 61, 65,
  73, 83-86,93-94, 139-141,
  147, 174, 184
Caulfield, Joan, 147
Caulfield, Phoebe, 57, 86, 90-
  92, 139, 153, 190
Caulfield, Vincent, 37, 39, 84
Celibacy, 12, 136
Chaplin, Charlie, 142-143
Cheever, John, 23, 63, 66
Christian Science Church, 132,
  177
Christian Science Monitor, 87
Chumley's, 56, 58, 59
City University of New York,
  125
Clarkson, Michael, 163

Cogdin, Don, 58
Collier's magazine, 25-26, 31,
  36, 39, 58, 84
Columbia University, 14, 22,
  23, 26-28, 83, 107, 182
*The Complete Uncollected Short
  Stories Of J.D. Salinger*, 160
Concentration camps, 11, 41,
  42, 54
Connolly, Steve, 164
Cornish, NH, 9, 81, 103-
  105,107-111, 113-114,
  116, 117, 129, 130, 136,
  140, 144, 147 150, 155,
  157, 159, 161-163, 175,
  176, 180, 181, 191
Cosmopolitan magazine, 59, 61
Counter Intelligence Corps, 33,
  38, 39, 49, 51, 52
Coutrell, Lane, 119
Cowley, Malcolm, 47
Czapnik, Dana, 95

D

D-Day: See Normandy
Dachau, 41
Dartmouth College, 111, 152,
  157, 175, 176, 181
"De Daumier-Smith's Blue
  Period," 97
Didion, Joan, 123
Douglas, Claire, 41, 108-115,
  117, 136, 141, 145, 155,

157, 159, 172, 176, 179, 182
Douglas, Jean, 109
Douglas, Robert Langdon, 109
Dowd, Maureen, 150
"Down at the Dinghy," 74, 96, 118, 119,153
Dream Catcher, 172, 173, 180

E
Eagleson, Janet, 150
Eddy, Mary Baker, 177
"Elaine," 27, 63, 141
Electric Literature, 94
Elfin, Mel, 105, 157, 158
Eppes, Betty, 163
Esquire, 25, 26, 31, 160

F
Fadiman, Clifford, 86
Faison, William, 17
Fat Lady, 122, 137
Faulkner, William, 29-30
Fiction Writers Handbook, 28
Fitzgerald, F. Scott, 17, 25, 32, 37, 60, 105
Fitzgerald, Paul, 38
Fleischmann, Raoul, 75
Foley, Martha, 22, 27
"For Esme – With love and Squalor," 43, 45, 49, 60, 69-72, 96, 97, 99, 100, 101, 139, 156, 180, 190

Fosburgh, Lacey, 161
"Franny," 10, 21, 76, 77, 110, 117, 119, 120-122, 124, 138
Franny and Zooey, 79, 104, 108,122, 124, 137, 138, 140, 153, 158, 189, 190
French, Warren, 93, 121, 123, 129
From Here to Eternity, 83

G
Gallagher, Bess, 117
Gibbs, Wolcott, 63
"A Girl I Knew," 20, 42, 118
Giroux, Robert, 84-85
Gladwaller, Babe, 32, 35, 37, 39, 45, 48
Glass, Buddy, 38, 127, 128, 138, 189
Glass, Les, 117
Glass, Seymour, 43, 44, 66, 67, 77, 79, 96, 100, 122, 127-129, 137, 140, 189
Glassmoyer, Franny, 21
"Go See Eddie," 25
Goddard College, 114
Good Housekeeping, 20, 118
The Gospel of Sri Ramakrishna, 112, 133, 134, 191
Gotham Book Mart, 155, 160, 169
Grant, Jane, 73

The Great Gatsby, 17, 38, 95, 125

Grunwald, Henry Anatole, 140

The Guardian, 10, 181, 183, 186

H

Hadley, Leila, 57, 62, 111

Hamilton, Hamish, 85, 100, 101, 133

Hamilton, Ian, 52, 93, 151, 164-171

Hamilton, Jamie, 101, 107, 164

Hamlet, 95, 171

Havemann, Ernest, 159

"The Hang of It," 26

Hand, Learned (Judge), 107, 111, 130, 164, 165

"Hapworth 16, 1924," 79-82, 131, 137, 187, 190

Harborough Publishing, 101

Harcourt Brace, 84-85

Harper's, 99, 100, 118, 139

Harvard Business School, 109

Harvard Law School, 165

Harvard University, 85, 93, 125, 176, 177

Hassan, Ihab, 119, 188

"The Heart of a Broken Story," 26

Heinemann, 167

Hemingway, Ernest, 19, 36-38, 43, 47, 58, 63, 106, 164

Hersey, John, 76

Hicks, Granville, 189

Highet, Gilbert, 100

Hinduism, 11, 79, 110, 117, 132, 133, 185

Hitler, Adolph, 40, 45, 50, 63

Hofco (J.S. Hoffman & Co.), 15, 18

Holden, William, 147

Holocaust, 20, 50, 54, 55

Hotchner, A.E., 58-59, 107

Hurtgen Forest, 39, 40, 42, 43, 48, 49

I

"I Went to School with Adolph Hitler," 63

"I'm Crazy," 84

In Search of J.D. Salinger, 52, 171

"The Inverted Forest," 61

J

Jesus prayer, 77, 120, 121

Jones, James, 83

Joyce, Elaine, 151

Joyce, James, 188

"Just Before the War with the Eskimos," 68

K

Kay Collyer and Boose, 168

Kakutani, Michiko, 80, 190

Kaufering Lager IV, 41, 42

Kazin, Alfred, 94, 123,188

Keenan, John, 36, 38,40-41, 50, 155, 185

Kennedy, Jackie, 174

Kennedy, John F., 174

Kennedy, John F., Jr, 181

Kerouac, Jack, 85

Kershaw, Alex, 39, 40

Kirsch, Adam, 140

Koan, 97

Kosner, Edward, 159

L

Lardner, Ring, 56

"The Last Day of the Last Furlough," 32, 37, 45

"The Laughing Man," 68

Leval, Pierre (Judge), 169,170

Levine, Paul, 88

Lewinsky, Monica, 150

Life magazine, 158

Lionel, 96, 100, 118, 139

Lippincott Company, 27

Little, Brown, 73, 85, 86, 87, 96, 115, 165

Lobrano, Gus, 66, 68, 69, 72, 73, 74-75,76, 77

"The Long Debut of Lois Taggert," 25

Lowell, Robert, 164

M

Mademoiselle magazine, 141

"The Magic Foxhole," 34

Mailer, Norman, 23, 26, 125-126, 187

Malamud, Bernard, 10, 11, 27, 187

Malcolm, Janet, 124-125

Massachusetts General Hospital, 177

Maugham, Somerset, 132

Maxwell, William, 64, 65, 66, 68, 69, 72, 77, 78, 86

Maynard, Joyce, 145, 146-150, 152, 153, 180

McBurney School, 15-16

McCarthy, Mary, 123

"Men Without Hemingway," 63

Menand, Louis, 93, 125

Miller, Jean, 143-144

Miner, Roger (Judge), 170

Mitchell, Michael, 85-86, 174

Mizener, Arthur, 99

Mockler, Jr., Colman, 109-110, 111

"Monologue for a Watery Highball," 63

Morgan Library and Museum, 84, 135

Murray, Elizabeth, 17-18, 31, 38, 43, 47, 60, 142,143, 156, 164, 165

N

NYU, 18, 21, 23
The Nation, 87
Nazis, 11, 19, 33, 41, 42,45, 48, 49, 50, 51, 54, 55, 60, 71, 108, 118
New England College, 175
New Republic magazine, 87
New York magazine, 81, 170
New York Observer, 172
New York Post, 159, 164
New York Social Register, 85
New York Times, 19, 44, 80, 83, 87, 100, 123, 127, 138, 145, 150, 161, 162, 170, 187, 190
The New Yorker, 21, 31, 58, 61, 63-82, 84, 92, 96, 97, 101, 108, 110, 111, 112, 119, 120, 121,123, 125,126, 128, 147,155, 158, 159, 186, 189, 190
Newman, John (Judge), 170
Newsweek, 105, 157,158, 162
Niagara Falls Review, 163
Nikhilananda (Swami), 134, 135, 137

Nine Stories, 44, 79, 96, 97, 99, 100,101-103, 117, 118, 137,139, 140, 187
Normandy (D-Day), 11, 33-35, 41, 44, 83

O

O'Hara, John, 63
O'Neill, Colleen, 116, 141,151-153, 183, 186
(See also: Salinger, Colleen O'Neill)
O'Neill, Eugene, 142
O'Neill, Oona, 142-143
Ober (Harold) Literary Agency, 25, 81
The Observer, 102, 167
Olding, Dorothy, 25, 64, 68
"Once a Week Won't Kill You," 26
Oxenberg, Catherine, 151
Oxford University, 85, 176-177

P

PBS documentary, 143, 145, 191
1133 Park Avenue, 15
Pattanaik, Dipti, 137
Paul, Marcia, 169
Pencey Prep, 16, 17, 65, 84, 88
Penguin Books, 101
Perelman, S.J., 111, 113

"A Perfect Day for Bananafish,"
43, 44, 61, 65-67, 74, 77,
96, 97, 121, 127, 137, 180
Perkins, Maxwell, 105
Poore, Charles, 44, 100
Prescott, Orville, 127, 129
Princeton University, 23, 34,
119, 165, 182, 187
Public School 166, 14-15

R
Radcliffe College, 109-110,
114
"Raise High the Roof Beam,
Carpenters," 77, 79, 112,
126-128, 137
Ramakrishna-Vivekananda
Center, 133-134, 135, 136
Random House, 164, 165,
166-169
Ransom Center, Univ. of Texas,
18
The Razor's Edge, 132
Reynal, Eugene, 85
Rochester Institute of
Technology, 114
Roeder, Bill, 162-163
Rogers Andy, 93-94
Ross, Harold, 73-75, 76
Ross Lillian, 76, 113, 156, 169
Roth, Philip, 10, 11, 187

S
Saint-Gaudens, Augustus, 104
Salerno, Shane, 143, 145, 191
Salinger, Colleen O'Neill, 116,
141, 151-153, 183, 186
(See also O'Neill, Colleen)
Salinger, Doris, 13, 16, 66,
103, 104, 111, 113, 115,
119, 158, 173
Salinger, J.D: A Writing Life,
164, 171
Salinger, Jerome David
Army service in U.S., 32-
46
Bar mitzvah, 10, 14, 15,
117
Boyhood, 13-17, 106
Children, 172-183
Columbia University, 22-
30
Death, 184-185
Depression, 42, 43-44, 62,
94, 132, 134
Marriage to Sylvia Welter
(1945-46), 51-54
Marriage to Claire Douglas
(1955-67), 110-114
Marriage to Colleen
O'Neill (1988-2010),
151-153
Schooling and college, 14-
18, 20-21, 22-30
Vienna life, 19-20

World War II service, 31-46
Salinger, Margaret (Peggy), 40-42, 51, 54, 78, 104, 107, 109, 112, 113, 114-115, 119, 130, 136, 147,148, 155-156, 172-183
Salinger, Matt, 9-10, 40, 41, 113, 114, 115, 136, 148, 172, 174, 175, 181-183, 184-185, 186
Salinger, Miriam, 14, 15, 111
Salinger, Sol, 14-16, 18, 21, 54, 66, 111, 117
San Francisco Journal, 22
Sappho, 126
Saturday Evening Post, 25, 31, 32, 35, 37, 160
Saybrook Institute, 114
"Scratchy Needle on a Phonograph Record," 59
Sergeant X, 44, 45 49, 70, 71-72, 96, 100
"Seymour, An Introduction," 78, 79, 128, 129-139, 131, 159, 187, 188
Shawn, William, 75-76, 78-79, 101, 113, 126, 128, 155, 156
Shields, David, 142, 191
Shipley School, 108
Simon, Neil, 151
"6 Rms Riv Vu," 151

Slawenski, Kenneth, 40, 130
Slicks, 25, 26, 31
"Slight Rebellion Off Madison," 58, 64
Smith, Bessie, 59
"Soft-Boiled Sergeant," 48
"Sonny, an Introduction," 158
Sotheby's, 149
Stars and Stripes, 74
Stork Club, 142
Steegmuller, Francis, 108
Stein, Beatrice, 108
Story magazine, 22, 23, 26, 27, 28, 31, 34, 141, 165
Story Press, 27
"The Stranger," 39, 43, 50

T
Tannenbaum, Boo Boo, 96, 118, 127
"Teddy," 96-100, 137, 139,140, 180, 190
Temple Emanu-El, 14
Theroux, Phyllis, 152
Thousand Island Park, 134
Time magazine, 93, 122, 140, 158
Times Literary Supplement, 170
Twain, Mark, 15

U
"Uncle Wiggily in Connecticut," 68, 153, 156, 157

University of Kansas, 26
Updike, John, 123, 124, 127, 138, 187, 189
Ursinus College, 20, 21, 23
Ursinus Weekly, 21

V
Valley Forge Military Academy, 16-17
Vedanta, 11, 12, 79, 80, 112, 117, 131, 132-137, 145, 158, 185, 190-191
The Veteran Who Is, the Boy Who Is No More, 94
Vienna, 19-20, 22, 23, 33, 42, 118
Viking Press, 85
Vivekananda Center, 134, 135, 136
Vivekananda (Swami), 134, 135, 136, 137
Vons Shops, 162

W
Washington Post, 81, 180
The Way of a Pilgrim, 110, 120, 121, 124
Weeks, Linton, 180
Welter, Sylvia, 51-54, 56, 110
Welty, Eudora, 100
White, E.B., 68-69, 75, 78
White, Katharine, 68-69, 77

Willkie, Wendell, 170
Wilson, Woodrow, 104
Windsor, VT, 103, 105, 144, 153, 163, 174
Woodburn, John, 85, 165
Woolf, Virginia, 188
World War I, 74, 132
World War II, 11, 39-46, 76, 100, 132, 165,184, 187
Wouk, Herman, 83

Y
Yagoda, Ben, 66, 189
Yale University, 119, 145-147, 180
Yeaton, Bertrand, 104-105, 157
"The Young Folks," 23-25, 139
"A Young Girl with No Waist at All," 141

Z
Zen Buddhism, 11, 56, 66, 67, 78, 80, 97, 99, 100, 102, 107, 110, 117, 126, 133, 144, 148, 191
"Zooey," 10, 37, 77-79, 104, 108, 117, 121-127, 131, 137-138, 140, 153,158, 187, 189-190

ACKNOWLEDGMENTS

This book is largely a work of analysis—synthesizing, redefining, and reinterpreting what is known of J. D. Salinger's reclusive life. It focuses on his personal experiences and his religious odyssey, from the Judaism of his youth to his embrace of Vedanta, a mystical form of Hinduism. And it casts a reflective light on his fiction, including some of the stories written before the one novel that made him famous. As such, I have drawn on the numerous scholarly papers and popular biographies published since *The Catcher in the Rye* in 1951.

I'm indebted to Kenenth Slawenski, who wrote a comprehensive biography of Salinger in 2010, just after Salinger died. Slawenski also runs a website called deadcaulfields.com, a fact-filled compendium of all things Salinger. Slawenski, in turn, tapped earlier work by other Salinger biographers, including Warren French (1963, revised in 1976), Ian Hamilton (1988), and Paul Alexander (1999), as well as memoirs written by one of Salinger's mistresses, Joyce Maynard (1998), and his daughter, Margaret Salinger (2000). (See Bibliography).

In addition, Shane Salerno and David Shields produced an encyclopedic book of interviews with people who knew Salinger or his work, rather like an oral history in print (2013). Much of it served as background material for their Salinger documentary on PBS.

Eberhard Alsen also deserves special mention. A German-born scholar who taught at the State University of New York, Alsen provided much significant detail on Salinger's time in Germany, during and after World War II. Among other things, he dug into German archives to answer many of the questions that surrounded Salinger's first marriage—a short-lived relationship after the war with a German ophthalmologist named Sylvia Welter. Alsen's 2018 study, *Salinger and the Nazis*, is a scholarly book written in plain English.

I'm very grateful to my agent, Lauren Eldridge (née Bittrich), formerly at the Lucinda Literary agency and now a book editor at Candlewick Press. Lauren made countless suggestions and landed the right publisher, Post Hill Press. At PHP, Alex Novak acquired the book, which was skillfully guided to the finish line by Caitlin Burdette, aided by copy editor Clayton Ferrell and others. At that point, Malka Margolies, a book industry veteran who runs her own communication firm, handled the publicity with verve and imagination.

Thanks, too, to many friends for their encouragement and suggestions: Kai Bird, Betsy Carter, Ron

Chernow, Kevin Cook, Myrna and Steve Greenberg, David Halpern, Lucinda Halpern, Christine Harper, Michael Kramer, Rocco Landesman, Eric Lax, Amal and Rene Malek, Lisa Napoli, Annie Navasky, Peter Osnos, Letty Cotton Pogrebin, Kathy Robbins, David Rudenstine, Anita and David Saunders, Margaret Sullivan, Kenny Turan, Sammy Wasson, Patty Williams, and Mary Willis.

As always, my wife, Lynn Povich, read versions of the manuscript along the way, offering numerous suggestions that improved the book's structure and content. An author herself (*The Good Girls Revolt*), she's the perfect first reader and partner.

Stephen B. Shepard
January 2024

ABOUT THE AUTHOR

Stephen B. Shepard is the founding dean emeritus of the Craig Newmark Graduate School of Journalism at the City University of New York. He served as a senior editor at *Newsweek*, the editor of *Saturday Review*, and editor-in-chief of *Business Week*. From 1992 to 1994, he was president of the American Society of Magazine Editors. Before teaching at CUNY, Shepard was a faculty member at the Columbia Journalism School, where he was co-founder and first director of the Knight-Bagehot Fellowships, a mid-career program for working journalists.

His book about journalism, *Deadlines and Disruption: My Turbulent Path from Print to Digital*, was published in 2012. His second book, published in 2018, is *A Literary Journey to Jewish Identity: Re-Reading, Bellow, Roth, Malamud, Ozick, and Other Great Jewish Writers*. And his most recent book is *Second Thoughts*, a series of essays published in 2021.

A native New Yorker, Shepard graduated from the Bronx High School of Science, then received his bachelor's degree from the City College of New York and his master's degree from Columbia University. He is married to Lynn Povich, author of *The Good Girls Revolt*, published in 2012. They have two children and two grandchildren.